Oh! Sing Praises!

BIBLICAL STUDIES ON PRAISE & WORSHIP

ANNETTE HUBBARD

outskirts
press

Outskirts Press, Inc.
http://www.outskirtspress.com

ISBN: 978-1-4787-1134-6

Outskirts Press and the "OP" logo are trademarks belonging to Outskirts Press, Inc.

PRINTED IN THE UNITED STATES OF AMERICA

This book is dedicated
To the memory
Of

Mother
Mrs. Josephine Woods
For her guidance and spiritual advice
to sing unto the Lord

&

Father
Mr. James H. Woods, Sr.
For his vivacious love of song and music

May 7, 2015

To My Sister in the Lord, Annette Hubbard:

I've known Annette for over 10 years and her love for worship is second to none! Her desire to bring the worshiper, choir member, worship pastor, praise leader, and the lay Christian alike to a greater understanding and appreciation on the subject of worship is seen in the attention to detail and sound Bible application in the pages of this book.

I believe this book and its contents could be a part of any seminary text book collection on this subject of praise and worship.

Keep up the good work, Annette and let the Lord bring glory and honor through you!

Pastor Kenneth J. Perdue
Counseling & Care Pastor
Abundant Living Family Church

Foreword

Oh! Sing Praises! is a stellar first book from worship leader, songwriter, Annette Hubbard. Annette gracefully takes us on a step-by-step journey through the essentials of God-honoring worship, combining Biblical foundations with practical application relevant to the day we live in. Twelve inspiring chapters cover a variety of topics, each rooted in unchanging scriptural principles.

Annette brings a clear understanding on how to become a passionate worshiper and how to develop an intimate relationship with God through worship. Every reader will be inspired to apply these truths into their daily living. Included is an in-depth study prepared specifically for the worship leader, choir member and front line singer. These chapters will equip the reader with foundational tools, bringing clarity and understanding to the purpose, reason, and benefits in worshiping in song, in spirit and in truth.

Oh! Sing Praises! is a must read for pastors, worship leaders, music directors, and anyone who wants to learn more about what it means to worship God, not only in song but through a variety of expressions, all bringing glory to God and drawing us closer to Him.

Louie Gutierrez
Worship Pastor
Abundant Living Family Church
Artist/Manager
GB5 – Gutierrez Brothers

Preface

We, as worshipers, were not created to carry problems, but created to carry "PRAISE". When praise is on our lips and a song in our hearts, we will experience a fulfilling relationship with God, and undoubtedly have answers to life.

Oh! Sing Praises! is a praise and worship devotional that teaches one how to become a passionate worshiper and how to have an intimate relationship with God. This book is an in-depth study of the Biblical principles of praise and worship that will help a worshiper stay committed to God, no matter what circumstances are encountered.

Why is this devotional different from any other? I explain in detail 12 descriptive words based on praise, in addition to many words that express worship. All are scripture-based and researched by the Strong's Concordance Dictionary. This book does not change the principles of praise and worship, but rather elevate ones awareness to a higher level of worship. I give answers to questions like: "What does it mean when we say, "Bless the Lord?" Or, "What does hallelujah really mean?" Praises to God are like keys that unlock doors to our lives, and praises bring harmony to a stressed, depressed life.

Many people have pre-conceived ideas about praise and worship, but have not been taught as to what are the true purposes of praise and worship. In this book, I allow the reader to become well acquainted with God, with such chapters as, "Praise and the Redemptive Names of God", or "Come Before His Presence". I also give the reader full detail about the old sacrificial system, "The Tabernacle of Moses", in comparison to the new sacrificial system, "The Tabernacle of Praise and Worship". Who is this Tabernacle of Praise and Worship? You, worshiper, are this tabernacle.

Many people also believe that worship is expressed only in song, but worship can be expressed in many ways. In the Worship Chapter, I discuss such topics as: "Worship in Prayer", "Worship in Warfare", "Worship in Healing", and much more.

Even though the emphasis of churches should heavily stem from the "Proclamation of the Gospel", a huge percentage of churches stem from one's perception and appearance of the well-inspiring voices of a choir, or dynamic praise and dance team. Oh! Sing Praises! is written to spiritually prepare the choir and praise dancers to obtain knowledge about worship and to understand why we sing and dance unto the Lord. Ultimately, when choir members understand the purpose of their calling, they become more effective in their presentation of song. With this in mind, there is a "Preaching to the Choir" section to assist the worshiper to sharpen their tools as they acknowledge who they are as anointed minstrels of God.

I've written this book as an accompaniment for choir orientation; to train, instruct, and edify the choir member. The "Journal of Selah", in the last chapter, can be used as a devotional to assist the worshiper in keeping maintenance of God's word in their heart, and a journal to write personal thoughts. This book can also be enjoyed by those who are in dance presentation.

As keys are used to unlock doors, worship unlocks "The Door of His Presence" and leads you to the realization of God's love. Once a person becomes a Christian, the next step is to become a worshiper, and once a worshiper, you can learn to become a doorkeeper, waiting at the entrance of God's Presence; listening for His Word. The Scriptures says,

For a day in Your courts is better than a thousand.
I would rather be a doorkeeper in the house of my God
Than dwell in the tents of wickedness.
Psalm 84:10

Let's enter through this Door and experience a wonderful place of worship. For in His Presence is fullness of joy, and at His right hand are pleasures forevermore!

Annette Hubbard
Email: abundanceofpraise@hotmail.com
Website: www.abundanceofpraiseministries.org

Acknowledgements

Praise and thanksgiving to my Heavenly Father, and Lord and Savior, Jesus Christ; the brightness of Your Presence and steadfastness of Your love has kept me focused all these years to bring to pass what you have placed in my heart; and for this I am grateful.

To Phylicia and Anita: you are the most beautiful daughters in the world, and you are God's gift to me. I rejoice every time I look upon your faces and see how God has blossomed you into the young ladies you are today. Your love and support has been the wind beneath my wings. I love you with all my heart.

My love and appreciation to my son-in-law, Jamaal and my heart jumps when I see my handsome grandson, LJ! Also introducing my new granddaughter, Ms. (Princess) Amani---------love those grandbabies!!!!

To my family, Warner and Doris Alexander, Barbara Jackson, and James Woods, Jr.; Wow, what a family! You believed that I could do it; you prayed that I could do it, and with God's help, I did it! Love you!

To my aunt, Ms. Mary L. McLennan – Mighty Mother of Zion! Your prayers and support have held up my arms, and encouraged me to stay in the race and never give up! Of course you know I'm your #1 niece!

To the best first cousins anyone could ever have – Ms. Jeannie Fells, when I see you, I see a rock; strong and secure in her Lord! Ms. Michelle Fells, "Mi, Prima!" Gloria a Dios! Thanks for your love and support!

To my Pastors Diego and Cindy Mesa at Abundant Living Family Church; thank you for the consistency in teaching and preaching the Gospel of Jesus Christ. Your lives are a testimony of the power of God and the power of His grace!

To Pastor Kenneth Perdue, Abundant Living Family Church – I count it a privilege and honor to have a pastor, who in accepting the call of ministry, serve God's people with commitment and faithfulness. Thank you for taking the time out of your busy schedule to read and review this book in clarity as it relates to the Biblical doctrine of God's Word, Amen!

To my first Choir Director, Mrs. Pamela Sigur – Thanks for the persistence in making us sing our parts over and over again until it was right, and most of all, thanks for teaching us to proclaim the ministry of the Gospel through song!

Thank you to Glenda Bridges for her love, prayers, and financial support. Her ministry, "Stubborn for a Reason" (Assertive Skills Training) is to help people become assertive not only in obtaining the promises of God, but also assertiveness in personal development. Stillsmallvoice.brdgs@gmail.com

Thank you to David Bridges for his editing expertise, and his ministry, Bridges Editing (djcurly84@yahoo.com). God bless you, my son!

Thank you to Christopher and Rosalind Liddell for your prayers and financial support. Your ministry, Angels Loft has been a blessing to the Body of Christ. Angels Loft, "The Mission and Goal of God's people; to Accept, to Embody and to Present the love of God." www.AngelsLoft.org

To the woman with the anointed touch of beauty, Ms. Monica Mullins. Thank you for hooking a sister up! You certainly know how to make all things beautiful in "His" time! Hair & Make-up Artistry By Monica, MakeupArtistrybyMonica@yahoo.com

To the lovely Kimberly Jones-Smith, and sister, Cynthia Shaw – Sweets are always brought to the table from your delicious delights! Thanks for your love and support! New Orleans Sweet Treats – Serving the only true Louisiana King Cake on the West Coast. www.neworleanssweettreats.com

To Mr. Oscar Easley and Dr. Terri Easley, thank you for your prayers and support. Your ministry, InTime Ministries (ITM) and ITM Health & Education Services (ITMHES), which is an HIV/AIDS Outreach, has been a blessing to the community by "Reaching God's People in Time." www.intimeministries.com

In appreciation, I'd like to thank Doris Alexander for her photography, and Miguel Benitez for his support. To all the ladies of Women Wonderfully Made ministries, and to Pastor Janet Flournoy of Women Mentoring Women ministries; I love you all, my sisters!

To family and friends that I may have not mentioned (you know who you are). Everyone who has touched my life has been a brick mortared and set into the building of my life; and the building keeps getting better and better!

And to all Praise and Worship Leaders, Praise Singers, Praise Dancers and Musicians throughout the world; your expression of ministry is appreciated!

To God Be the Glory!

Contents

Introduction

The central theme of the entire Bible is God's love demonstrated through the sacrifice of Jesus Christ; however, if we take an even closer look, we will see that God requires and loves the atmosphere of praise and worship.

Throughout this devotional, my objective is to communicate to the worshiper to spend quality time with God, and in addition, to validate those of you who are involved in praise and worship, whether you are a choir member, a praise dancer, a musician, or a soloist; your presence, your position, and your purpose make a difference in the Body of Christ.

Everyone is created to bring praise and glory to God! But those who are set apart to bring glory to God through praise and worship are specifically commissioned to usher the Presence of the Lord in the Sanctuary.

If you spend time in God's word, you will observe that God is a music lover. He loves singing. Did you know that God sings over you? Zephaniah 3:17 (KJV) says: The Lord thy God in the midst of thee is mighty; He will save, He will rejoice over thee with joy; He will rest in His love, He will joy over thee with singing. Sounds wonderful, doesn't it? Psalm 32:7 says that God will give you songs of deliverance, and in Mark 14:26, after Jesus had communion with His disciples, they sung a hymn. Where would this world be without a song?

The Bible commands us to sing praises to God:
Psalm 47:6 - *Sing praises to God, sing praises, sing praises to our King, sing praises* (KJV).

It doesn't matter if you have a melodious voice or not, God loves the heart of a worshiper who sings praises unto Him!

As a person who loves music too, I am attracted to my all-time favorite scripture in the entire Bible:

Psalm 104:33-34 (KJV)
I will sing unto the Lord as long as I live; I will sing praise to my God while I have my being. My meditation of Him will be sweet, I will be glad in the Lord.

This is an invitation to sit at the table with me and enjoy fellowship as together we talk about His wondrous works, and partake of the Bread of His Presence!

Annette

CHAPTER 1

Praise & The Redemptive Names of God

As we learn about praise and worship, one important fact is necessary: we must _know_ God in order to effectively praise God. The Name of the Lord represents His Presence and character. What does it mean to know God?

Daniel 11:32b
"......But the people who know their God shall be strong and carry out great exploits."

As you begin to know God and praise Him for who He is, you will become strong and experience Him on a deeper level in every area of your life. The word, _know_ is based on relationship, not ritualism.

Know, (yada), Strong's Concordance, #H3045
- To know intimately
- To acknowledge and know for certain
- To understand, observe, and perceive
- To be acquainted with

God's word tells us not to glory in the fact that we are wise, strong, or rich, but to glory in the fact that we "know" God.

Jeremiah 9:23-24

23) *Thus says the LORD; Let not the wise man glory in his wisdom, let not the mighty man glory in his might, nor let the rich man glory in his riches;*

24) *But let him who glories glory in this, that he understands and knows Me, that I am the LORD exercising lovingkindness, judgment, and righteousness in the earth. For in these I delight," says the LORD.*

What is **PRAISE**?

Praise is the expressed glorification of God.

Psalm 50:23

Whoever offers praise glorifies Me; and to him who orders his conduct aright, I will show the salvation of God.

To understand this scripture fully, I researched a few words in Hebrew to clarify its true meaning. Hold on and get ready, because once we break this scripture apart, you're *really* going to start praising God!

Breakdown		
Word	Strong's Concordance	Definition
Offers	# 2076 – Zabach	To slaughter or kill as a sacrifice. To bring an offering.
Praise	# 8426 – Todah	To extend the hand and call upon God; to openly acknowledge Who He is. To offer thanksgiving and praise as a sacrifice.
Glorifies	# 3513 – Kabad	To honor and exalt God who is glorious and very great in splendor and majesty; weighty and heavy in riches.
Orders	# 7760 – Soom, Seem	To commit, consider, & be determined to change.
Conduct	# 1870 – Derek	A course of life; a mode of action; a custom; conversation; a road or pathway.
Show	# 7200 – Ra'ah	To joyfully look upon; to gaze, to stare, to see.
Salvation	# 3468 – Yesha	Liberty, deliverance, prosperity, healing, salvation and safety.

This is a breakdown of this scripture:
Whoever offers thanksgiving and praise as a sacrifice glorifies God who is weighty in riches, honor, splendor, and majesty. And to him who is determined to change his mode of actions and conversation to that of praise, God will joyfully look upon him with liberty, deliverance, prosperity, healing, salvation, and safety!

God looks at our heart at all times, and in this particular Psalm, the Israelites were neither in the right frame of mind nor heart. For instance, their mouths got them in trouble by not keeping vows to God, and speaking evil against their neighbor. Their sacrifices were being offered ritualistically and without genuine efforts, it was of no value. God wanted a better sacrifice; a sacrifice of praise and thanksgiving! God wanted them to make a commitment to change.

What about us today? Can we change our conversation to praise and glorify God rather than our circumstances? Can we commit to order our actions rightly in being faithful to promises made to God and not speaking evil against our neighbors? Selah. (Pause and think of that).

We must kill our own actions, thoughts, and feelings, and take on the Word of God in faith and offer God a sacrifice of PRAISE! The Apostle Paul says this so eloquently in the scriptures:

Hebrews 13:15
"Therefore, by Him, let us continually offer the sacrifice of praise to God, that is, the fruit of our lips, giving thanks to His name."

The Prophet Habakkuk changed his perspective on life by not rejoicing in his circumstances, but rejoicing in the God of his salvation.

Habakkuk 3:17-19
17) *Though the fig tree may not blossom, nor fruit be on the vines; though the labor of the olive may fail, and the fields yield no food; though the flock may be cut off from the fold, and there be no herd in the stalls—*
18) *Yet I will rejoice in the LORD, I will **joy** in the God of my salvation.*
19) *The LORD is my strength; He will make my feet like deer's feet, and He will make me walk on my high hills.*

Verse 18 reflects Habakkuk's praises to God; I will rejoice in the LORD, I will joy in the God of my salvation. The word "joy" is the Hebrew word, "Giyl" pronounced, (gheel), (#H1523), which means to spin around and rejoice; be glad, and be joyful. It literally means "dancing for joy" or "leaping for joy". How can Habakkuk be joyful?

Even though the situation doesn't look good at all, Habakkuk is leaping for joy over his fellowship and relationship with God! He finds the true source of his joy in God and not his circumstances. And to put a cap on it, Habakkuk glorifies God by saying: "The LORD GOD is my strength; He will make my feet like deer's feet, and He will make me walk on my high hills".

What a praise!!

You, too, can take the high road by changing your conversation through glorifying God and not your problems; and guess what? God will show you His liberty, deliverance, prosperity, healing, salvation, and safety!

Amen!

The Redemptive Names of God

As stated previously, one must know God in order to praise God. The name, <u>LORD</u> is the Hebrew word YHWH (Yahweh), which means Jehovah, the Self-Existent and Eternal God. The title <u>Lord</u> means to be Master or Ruler, or to reign in authority. When we look at LORD in all caps, it is the Trinity of God; God the Father, God the Son, and God, the Holy Spirit. When Lord is in lower case as a title, it is one of the titles of Jesus Christ, as Master and Lord of all.

Another meaning of Lord is, "<u>The One who would redeem His people</u>." When we learn about His Redemptive Names, we learn more about His personality and how to respond to such an awesome God as He.

What is meant by "redemptive"?

Redeem
- To rescue from captivity or bondage
- To recover
- To deliver
- To purchase back
- To ransom

When Adam sinned, we became separated from God, but Jesus, The Christ, The Anointed One, paid the price for us to be purchased back to God. Jesus Christ delivered us from bondage and we do not have to pay for the penalty of sin. Hallelujah!

So when we're in trouble, all we have to do is believe and call on His Name. When we're in need of salvation, believe in His Name, Y'hoshua – Jehovah-Saves. When we're in need of healing; believe and call on His name, Jehovah Rapha; when we need victory, believe

8

and call on Jehovah Nissi; when we need peace, believe and call on Jehovah Shalom. In other words, call on Him and Praise Him!!!!

When you praise God in the fullness of His name, you personally become aware of God and experience Him on a deeper level. When you praise God through knowing Him and His personality, you begin to glorify Him, exalt Him, and honor Him. God will make Himself known and you will receive strength to overcome any difficulty.

The following are a few of the Redemptive Names of God:

JEHOVAH JIREH – Genesis 22:1-19
The LORD God Will Provide –

God made a promise to Abraham that He would have a son. After many years, God kept His promise and Abraham and Sarah miraculously had Isaac in their old age. However, one day Abraham's faith was tested when God told him to offer his only son as a sacrifice (a burnt offering).

As Abraham obeyed God and traveled up the mountain, Isaac asked his father, "where is the lamb for a burnt offering?" Abraham's response was, "God Himself will provide the lamb for the burnt offering, my son." As you read the story, Abraham did not have to kill his son, and God provided a "ram in the bush".

God made a promise to multiply Abraham's descendants as the stars of heaven. As a result of not withholding his son, Abraham's generations were blessed. Read Genesis 21:12 and Hebrews 11:17-19.

In relation to today's economic rise of gasoline prices, real estate deflation and unemployment, our faith, can be tested. However, in the trial of testing, don't withhold your praises to God! He will bless and make provision for you through the promises of His Word. The LORD is Jehovah Jireh, and He is LORD over your provision! Amen!

JEHOVAH RAPHA – Exodus 15:22-27
The LORD God Who Heals –

As the Children of Israel were leaving Egypt, they came to a place called the Desert of Shur. In this particular place, they could not drink the water because it was bitter; if they drank the waters, they would become ill. Instead of praising God, the people complained. As Moses cried out to the LORD, he was shown a piece of wood. Moses was told to throw the wood in the water. As a result of his obedience, the waters became sweet. God made a promise of healing to the Children of Israel.

Exodus 15:26
"And said, 'If you diligently heed the voice of the LORD your God and do what is right in His sight, give ear to His commandments and keep all His statutes, I will put none of the diseases on you which I have brought on the Egyptians. For I am the LORD who <u>heals</u> you.'"

The Name Jehovah Rapha means:
- To cure
- To heal
- To repair
- To mend
- To restore health

The wood that Moses threw in the water is a representation of Jesus who would die on a wooden cross for our sins. Jesus said in Luke 4:18, "The Spirit of the Lord is upon Me...............He has sent Me to heal." Jesus paid a dear price for your healing, and He bore your sins on a tree.

1 Peter 2:24

"Who Himself bore our sins in His own body on the tree, that we, having died to sins, might live for righteousness—by whose stripes you were healed."

There you have it; Old and New Testament evidence that He is Jehovah Rapha, the LORD God who heals you. Are you sick in your body? Has this sickness made you bitter? Begin to praise God; He will turn your bitterness into something sweet.

JEHOVAH NISSI – Exodus 17:8-15
The LORD God, your Banner & Victory –

The symbol of a banner being lifted meant that the people were called for battle, meeting, or instructions. In this particular passage, the banner was lifted to call for battle against the Amalekites. Moses said to Joshua, (verse 9), "Choose some of our men to fight and tomorrow I will stand on top of the hill with the staff of God in my hands." This was the same staff that Moses used to perform miracles in Egypt. Pay close attention to verse 11:

Exodus 17:11 (NIV)
"As long as Moses held up his hands, the Israelites were winning, but whenever he lowered his hands, the Amalekites were winning."

Note:
The power was not in the staff; the power came from the Throne of the LORD as Moses lifted his hands toward God.

Exodus 17:16 (NIV)
"He said, 'For hands were lifted up to the Throne of the LORD. The LORD will be at war against the Amalekites from generation to generation.'"

As we praise God and our hands are lifted to the Throne, we win!!! And just like Moses was on top of the hill with the staff of God in his hands, we must be on top of our game with the Word of God in our hands and also on our lips, giving God the sacrifice of praise as Jehovah Nissi our victory!

What are you doing with your hands? Are you striking your enemy, or are you lifting your hands to the Almighty God who has all power in His hands? Think about it, as you praise God and lift your hands to Him, it is a sign of the Banner of the Lord, the place of victory! Amen!

JEHOVAH SHALOM – Judges 6:24
The LORD God of Peace –

The Children of Israel were oppressed by their enemies due to their disobedience to God, and they were not living in peace, but frustration. In desperation, they cried out to the Lord, and God sent them a deliverer, whose name was Gideon. An interesting fact is that Gideon didn't view himself as a deliverer. The insecurities of himself and many others made them hide in caves from their enemies.

With a sense of abandonment, Gideon questions whether the God of Israel is with him. Well, God appears to him as the Angel of the LORD, and says, "The LORD is with you, you mighty man of valor!" In addition, the Angel reveals that Gideon is the one to be used to bring about deliverance for His people (Judges 6:12-14). After Gideon realizes that he has spoken with the Angel of the Lord, he thinks he is going to die, but the Angel of the LORD offers him peace.

Judges 6:23 (NKJV)
Then the LORD said to him, "Peace be with you; do not fear, you shall not die."

Shalom in its fullest expression means:

- Wholeness
- Security
- Well-being
- Prosperity
- Friendship

Jehovah Shalom was offering Gideon wholeness, security, and well-being in replacement of depression and intimidation; and because of this peace, he was able to overcome his enemies. Are you full of insecurities and despair? Are you frustrated with who you are, and hiding from life? Do not be afraid, Jehovah Shalom is with you! His mercy and grace shall give you peace, wholeness, well-being, prosperity and friendship with God.

JEHOVAH ROHI – Psalm 23, Isaiah 40:11
The LORD God your Shepherd –

As sheep are under the total care and protection of the shepherd, so are you under the total care and protection of Jesus, the Great Shepherd. By reciting Psalm 23, you will experience God's freshness in times of stress and turmoil. A sense of well-being will overtake you as He makes you to lie down in green pastures and leads you beside quiet waters. Isaiah 40:11 is another passage that depicts serenity and protection.

Isaiah 40:11 (NKJV)
"He will feed His flock like a shepherd; He will gather the lambs with His arms, and carry them in His bosom, and gently lead those who are with young."

The NIV translation says......*"He gathers the lambs in His arms, and carries them close to His heart."*

Isn't it comforting to know that Jehovah Rohi is your shepherd? The next time you are stressful, take a deep breath and praise the LORD God, your Shepherd. He will draw you close to His heart and will guide you to places of rest.

JEHOVAH T'SIDKENU – Jeremiah 23:5-6, Isaiah 61:10
The LORD God your Righteousness –

Jesus, the King of Righteousness, shall reign and prosper both now and forever and we can greatly rejoice in Him as the God of our salvation.

Jeremiah 23:5-6
5) "Behold, the days are coming," says the LORD, "That I will raise to David a Branch of righteousness; a King shall reign and prosper, and execute judgment and righteousness in the earth.
6) In His days Judah will be saved, and Israel will dwell safely; now this is His name by which He will be called:

THE LORD OUR RIGHTEOUSNESS

Isaiah 61:10
I will greatly rejoice in the LORD, my soul shall be joyful in my God; for He has clothed me with the garments of salvation, He has covered me with the robe of righteousness.

Praise God and rejoice in the works of Jesus Christ because He has allowed us to have a right relationship with God through His blood! Amen!

JEHOVAH SHAMMAH – Ezekiel 48:35
The LORD God who is There – or
(The LORD God who is Present)

Ezekiel 48:35
"All the way around shall be eighteen thousand cubits, and the name of the city from that day shall be THE LORD IS THERE."

This passage speaks of the earthly and heavenly restoration of the Lord's people in the city of Jerusalem; however, we can also praise God and know that He is here for His people.

We can praise Him, because He is the Lord whose name alone is Jehovah, and He is true and faithful to His people. He is rich in mercy, glorious in majesty, and righteous in judgment. He is wise and holy to defend and prosper His people; and in His presence is fullness of joy! This is the statement of faith for every believer that can say, Jehovah Shammah, "My God is present!"

And until that day when we come to the gates of Heaven, where light and love flows from the Throne of God, we can rejoice with blissful glee and say, "THE LORD IS PRESENT!"

JEHOVAH M'KADDESH - Leviticus 20:7-8
The LORD God Who Sanctifies –

When we accept Jesus Christ as our personal savior, we become righteous and holy unto the Lord; however, once we make a decision to consecrate ourselves and "live" holy, Jehovah M'Kaddesh is the One who sanctifies us; we cannot do this on our own. Consecration sets us apart for the Lord, and as we do, God is our means of sanctification, as He sets us aside for His use, and His use only. Leviticus 20:8 says, "I am the LORD who sanctifies you."

We cannot obey God on our own, His name, Jehovah M'Kaddesh, literally means, "The One who sanctifies you to obey Him." All that is required on our part is worship to Him, and He will do the sanctification. The Bible reveals how Jehovah M'Kaddesh sanctifies us: through

15

the daily devotion of His Word. The reading and application of His Word cleanse and wash away our former life and show us how to live a new created life in Christ Jesus. **Ephesians 5:26.**

Are you having a hard time obeying God? Is it hard for you to resist the desires of the flesh? Praise and worship to Jehovah M'Kaddesh will cause you to yield to the will of God, and in turn, the God of Peace will preserve you blameless; not just some of you, but all of you— your <u>spirit</u>, <u>soul</u>, and <u>body</u>. **1 Thessalonians 5:23**

CHAPTER 2

Come Before His Presence

"...Make a sanctuary for me, and I will dwell among them."
Exodus 25:8 (NIV)

God's desire is to have a close relationship through love, fellowship and interaction with mankind; however, in the Old Testament, God was very strict when the Children of Israel came before His presence. For instance, upon Moses receiving the Ten Commandments, specific instructions were given to the Children of Israel; that neither them nor any animal touch or come near the mountain of God or the results was death.

In fact, in order to have your sins forgiven, you had to follow certain rules and regulations, such as the offering of the blood of bulls and goats as a substitute for your sins. The reason for this was that God is holy, and you could not just haphazardly come into His presence; <u>a sacrifice had to be made.</u> (Read Leviticus, chapters 1-4).

God's answer for longing to be with His people was a plan for Moses to build a tabernacle. The word "<u>*tabernacle*</u>" means "<u>*dwelling place*</u>"; and it was through this dwelling place that God connected with His people.

"Then I will dwell among the Israelites and be their God. They will know that I am the Lord their God, who brought them out of Egypt so that I might dwell among them." Exodus 29:45-46 (NIV)

It is believed that the tabernacle was first erected in the wilderness exactly one year after the Passover when the Israelites were freed from their Egyptian slavery (circa 1450 BC). The tabernacle was a mobile unit with portable furniture that traveled with the people on their journeys. God guided them from place to place as a pillar of cloud by day and a pillar of fire by night.

When they were instructed to stop at a particular place, the 12 tribes would set up camp according to tribe with the tabernacle in the center. This is a great illustration expressing that worship should be at the center of our lives. Specifications had to be followed, not only in the structure of the tabernacle, but also in the way the Israelites worshipped. Any irreverence or ritual uncleanness could result in death.

In Leviticus 10, Nadab and Abihu (Aaron's sons) died before the LORD because of the way they worshipped by offering strange fire. Why did they die? Ancient Jewish interpretation reveals that Nadab and Abihu were drunk, and the fire that was offered was strange, idolatrous worship, and not worship to God. Nadab and Abihu came before the presence of God not honoring God, but honoring a lifestyle of drunkenness and idolatry.

Leviticus 10:3
And Moses said to Aaron, "This is what the LORD spake, saying: 'By those who come near Me, I must be regarded as holy; And before all the people I must be glorified'."

What are we offering to God in our praise and worship? Are we offering hearts of humility? Are we honoring God with a lifestyle of holiness, or is it a lifestyle strange to God because we give others or our possessions first place in our lives instead of spending time with Him? Selah.

The main emphasis of our worship must focus on God in His glorification, not on our own way of idolatrous worship.

Come before His presence; honor Him; respect Him; He, alone, must be glorified. ·

If anyone speaks, let him speak as the oracles of God. If anyone ministers, let him do it as with the ability which God supplies, that in all things God may be glorified through Jesus Christ, to whom belong the glory and the dominion forever, and ever.
Amen.
1 Peter 4:11

CHAPTER 3

The Tabernacle of Moses (The Old Sacrificial System)

<u>The Tabernacle of Moses</u> was a symbol of worship and fellowship with God. Everything in this tabernacle points to Jesus Christ; in fact each article of furniture is a representation of Jesus. Even the position of the furniture from an aerial view makes the symbol of a cross.

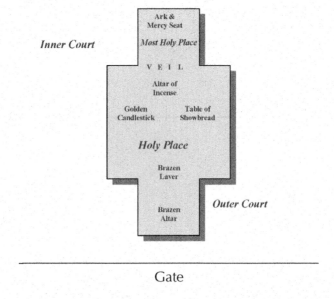

Gate

Let's take a quick study of all of the articles of furniture

Keep in mind that the Children of Israel were being introduced to God's system of worship that allowed them to have a relationship with Him through the Tabernacle. Within this Tabernacle, the emphasis is on being one with God, "Atonement". The High Priest made atonement for the Children of Israel once a year.

The Tabernacle had an Outer Court, which consisted of the entry Gate, the Brazen Altar and the Brazen Laver; an Inner Court, which is the Holy Place, consisted of the Golden Candlestick, the Table of Showbread, and the Altar of Incense. The Most Holy Place or Holy of Holies contained the Ark of the Covenant and the Mercy Seat.

GATE
The worshipper entered into this gate with a sacrifice. Today we enter the presence of God through the gate, which is Jesus Christ. Jesus says in John 10:9 – "I am the door. If anyone enters by Me, he will be saved and will go in and out and find pasture." Jesus also says in John 14:6, "I am The Way, The Truth, and The Life, no man comes to the Father accept through Me."

We are the righteousness of God in Christ Jesus, and because of this, we can enter into His gates with thanksgiving, and into His courts with praise!!!

BRAZEN ALTAR
The Brazen Altar was a huge piece of furniture that was square in shape and had horns at each corner. The priest would take the sacrifice and kill it at the Brazen Altar. The word "sacrifice" means to kill or slaughter for a purpose. After the animal was killed, the blood was shed on the horns of the altar, and the animal was burned with fire. Praise God for the precious blood of Jesus who was offered as a sacrificial lamb for our sins, and without the shedding of blood, there is no remission of sin.

As we relate to this today, the Brazen Altar is a place to surrender to God, and die to our flesh. The Bible says that no flesh should glory in His presence. (1 Corinthians 1:29)

Therefore, when we praise God, it requires the death of our flesh. Our flesh represents the soul realm; the mind, will, and emotions. As we praise God by glorifying Him, it doesn't matter what we think, how we feel, or what it looks like—what matters is our faith in GOD and the sacrifice of praise coming forth from our mouths!!!

BRAZEN LAVER

After killing the sacrifice, the priest washed at the Brazen Laver. The priest's feet were defiled by constant contact with the earth and their hands defiled by contact with the sacrifice; therefore, they had to wash at the Brazen Laver before ministry to God in the Holy Place.

The Brazen Laver is also called the place of sanctification. Sanctification means to be "set apart" for use. At this point, we can praise God for Jesus, who sanctifies us through the truth of His Word and by the washing of water through the daily application of His word.

John 17:17
"Sanctify them by Your truth. Your word is truth."

Ephesians 5:26b
"…Cleansing her by the washing of the water through the word."

After cleansing, the priests were clothed with priestly garments and anointed to enter the Holy Place. (Exodus 30:19-21 and Leviticus 29:4-7)

As part of our sanctification, we must kill those things that are not like God, and praise God for the righteousness that has been obtained through the blood of Jesus Christ. We can then put on the garment of salvation and the garment of praise and worship God in the Holy Place.

Purge me with hyssop, and I shall be clean; wash me and I shall be whiter than snow. Create in me a clean heart, O God, and renew a steadfast spirit within me.

Psalms 51:7, 10

THE HOLY PLACE

These things existed in the Holy Place: The Golden Candlestick; the Table of Showbread; The Golden Altar of Incense, and the Veil. All of which point to Jesus Christ, and again, we should give the attention of our praise to Him.

- *Golden Candlestick*

Because the Holy Place was covered, the Golden Candlestick was used as the only light for the priests. Pressed olives were used to make pure oil for the lamps to burn. The significance here is that the oil is a symbol of the Holy Spirit, and we can definitely praise Jesus who says, "I am the Light of the World; he who follows Me shall not walk in darkness, but have the light of life" - John 8:12. Again the Word of God says in 2 Samuel 22:29, "For You are my lamp, O LORD; the LORD shall enlighten my darkness."

- *The Table of Showbread –*

The Table of Showbread, also called the Bread of His Presence, serves as a symbol of God's word, and His provision. Twelve loaves were made of pierced bread and was to be replaced every Sabbath. This bread was only to be eaten by the priest; it sustained them while ministering, and it was to be evenly lined in two rows, symbolizing alignment of our lives with the word of God. Jesus, our High Priest, proclaimed, "I am the Bread of Life," John 6:48. And even as this bread was pierced, Jesus was pierced on the cross

23

for our sins. Guess what? Jesus also says He is Lord of the Sabbath, Mark 2:28.

- *The Altar of Incense* -
Whereas the Bronze Altar filled the air with the aroma of a dead animal sacrifice, the Altar of Incense filled the air with sweet-smelling incense. No offerings were burnt on this altar; it was reserved exclusively for the burning of incense each morning and evening. Incense is symbolic for prayer and worship. One other thing is symbolic about this altar—it represents the prayers and intercession of Jesus. Hebrews 7:25 says that Jesus lives to make intercession for us, and Isaiah 53:12 says that Jesus poured His soul out unto death, and made intercession for the transgressors.

- *The Veil* -
A veil separated the Holy Place from the Most Holy Place. This veil was the last thing seen before entering the Holy of Holies; and it was only permitted for the priests to go behind the veil into the Presence of God once a year. In Matthew 27:51, Jesus (being our High Priest) was dying on the cross and feeling the pain of separation from God, the Bible says He cried out with a loud voice and yielded up His spirit. At this point, the veil of the temple was torn in two from top to bottom. Just like the veil opened the way to the Presence of God in the Most Holy Place, Jesus' death efficaciously opened the way to the presence of God to salvation! Amen!

THE MOST HOLY PLACE – HOLY of HOLIES
- THE ARK OF THE COVENANT
The Ark of the Covenant (Exodus 25:10) signified the dwelling place of the Presence of God in The Holy of Holies. Specifically, the Ark was a chest, which was made of wood, covered in pure gold. According to Hebrews 9:4, within this Covenant were three (3) things:
1. The Golden Pot (which contained Manna): A type of Christ

2. Aaron's rod that budded, symbolizing that Aaron was chosen by God as High Priest, and symbolic of the Resurrection of Christ
3. Tables of the Covenant: The Ten Commandments (God's Laws)

The Ark accompanied the children of Israel on their journeys through the wilderness. The Ark was placed in the "Holy of Holies", and as previously mentioned, and the High Priest made atonement for the Children of Israel once a year. It was a very sacred place.

As the Ark of the Covenant had these three things inside of it, symbolically, as a worshiper, we should have the same things inside of us:
- Feeding on God's Word (manna)
- Acknowledging Jesus as our Great High Priest, and having His resurrection power in our lives (Aaron's bud)
- Respecting and acknowledging those in authority. (Aaron's rod)
- The maintenance of God's Word (laws) in our heart.

The Ark of the Covenant represented God's authority, His direction, and His love for the Children of Israel. God wants to come into the inner most part of our hearts, and allow His Presence to permeate our souls and receive His love and direction.

I will put My law in their minds, and write it on their hearts; and I will be their God, and they shall be My people.
Jeremiah 31:33

- THE MERCY SEAT -

The Mercy Seat, which is symbolic of God's Throne, is a lid of pure gold at top of the Ark, and is used as a cover. Two Cherubim Angels are on top of the Mercy Seat, with their wings spread, looking down. They are specifically looking down at Jesus' blood that was sprinkled on the Mercy Seat.

Did you know that the Ark of the Covenant is in your future? When we get to Heaven, we shall finally see the glorious manifestation of God's Throne.

Then the temple of God was opened in heaven, and the Ark of His Covenant was seen in His temple, and there were lightnings, noises, thundering, and earthquakes and great hail.
Revelation 11:19

CHAPTER **4**

The Tabernacle of Praise & Worship
(The New Sacrificial System)
(The Worshiper)

<u>**Today's Worship**</u>

Our worship today does not require the blood sacrifice of bulls and goats. Jesus Christ was the propitiation for our sins, which means He appeased the wrath of God, and sin was totally eradicated by the sacrifice of His life. Thereby, we have access to the Throne of God through the righteous works of Jesus' blood, and we now bring to God the sacrifice of praise, the fruit of our lips, and the offering of our lives. This is why we come straight through the gate with praise and thanksgiving for the completed work at Calvary.

Enter in His gates with thanksgiving, and into His courts with praise!
Psalm 100:4

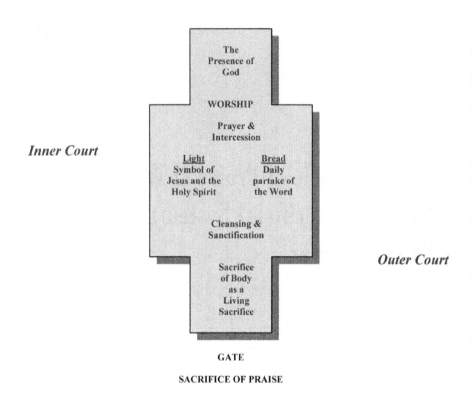

Inner Court

The
Presence of
God

WORSHIP

Prayer &
Intercession

Light
Symbol of
Jesus and the
Holy Spirit

Bread
Daily
partake of
the Word

Cleansing &
Sanctification

Sacrifice
of Body
as a
Living
Sacrifice

Outer Court

GATE

SACRIFICE OF PRAISE

The Tabernacle of Praise & Worship is not an actual tabernacle in the Bible, but guess what? "YOU" are actually this tabernacle.

As previously stated, under the Old Sacrificial System, a sacrifice was made with a dead animal, but God does not want a dead sacrifice any longer. The New Sacrificial System requires a "live" sacrifice: a living sacrifice of our lives given to God to be used for His service.

Both Old and New Sacrificial Systems require three (3) things:
   1) Requires – A sacrifice
   2) Requires – A priest
   3) Requires – A worshiper

Let's discover in detail what these requirements are all about.

1) Sacrifice
- A Sacrifice of Praise – Hebrews 13:15

Upon entrance of the Tabernacle of Praise & Worship, we offer the sacrifice of PRAISE.

Hebrews 13:15
Therefore by Him let us continually offer the sacrifice of praise to God, that is, the fruit of our lips, giving thanks to His name.

You may not feel like praising God continually, however, the Bible specifically tells us how to begin this sacrifice of praise: With singing and thanksgiving!!!!!! Yes, singing!!! Singing is the vehicle that will help us praise God with passion and vibrancy; and thanksgiving is the gateway to praise.

Psalm 100:1-2, 4
Make a joyful shout to the LORD, all you lands!
Serve the LORD with gladness, Come before His presence with singing.
Enter into His gates with thanksgiving and unto His courts with praise.

As we enter into this new tabernacle, we enter the gate:
- With singing
- With thanksgiving
- With praise

What is all this singing and praising about? The Bible says we should make a joyful shout; why? The basis of this joyful shout is that we are celebrating Jesus Christ, who was and is the sacrificial Lamb of God who takes away the sins of the world. We are celebrating His blood-shed, His love, His mercy, and His forgiveness of sins. No more do we have to continually bring a dead sacrifice to God, our sacrifice is alive with praise!

In fact, throughout this Tabernacle of Praise & Worship, we can sing songs of praise at each article:

- Gate – Songs of thanksgiving and praise
- Brazen Altar – Songs of praise of forgiveness & righteousness
- Brazen Laver – Songs of praise in sanctification
- Golden Candlestick – Songs of Jesus as the Light of the world & songs of the fire of the Holy Spirit
- The Table of Showbread – Songs of Jesus as the Bread of Life, The Word of God, and songs of provision
- The Altar Of Incense – Songs of prayer and intercession
- The Ark of the Covenant & Mercy Seat – Worship songs of love and adoration to God

As the Tabernacle of God, Ephesians 5:18-19 says we should be filled with the Spirit, speaking to one another in psalms and hymns and spiritual songs, singing and making melody in our hearts to the Lord.

- A Living Sacrifice – Romans 12:1

The other type of sacrifice in the Tabernacle of Praise and Worship is a Living Sacrifice, which is the sacrifice of our bodies to God. You may ask what does this have to do with worship. Let's look at what Romans has to say:

Romans 12:1 (NIV)
*Therefore, I urge you, brothers, in view of God's mercy, to offer your bodies as living sacrifices, holy and pleasing to God—this is your **spiritual act of worship.***

Note from The Living Bible:
A Living Sacrifice - Since Christians (both Jews and Gentiles) are the new people of God, the "New Israel," then should we not offer sacrifices to God, just as the Old Testament Jews did? Yes, but not animal sacrifices at the temple of Jerusalem; rather we should offer our bodies (all that we are) as "living sacrifices" each day to God.

2) A Priest

After a sacrifice was made, it was given to the priest to minister in the Holy Place and the Holy of Holies, likewise Jesus became our Great High Priest. As you present your body as a sacrifice, you become a priest and minister in the Holy Place. The Bible says in 1 Peter 2:9, that we are a royal priesthood that proclaim His praises! Revelation 1:6 – Jesus has also made us kings and priests.

As a priest in the Holy Place, we fellowship with Jesus who is the Light of the World and the fire of the Holy Spirit as He purges and purifies our hearts, as well as partake of the Bread of His Presence, feasting on the Word of God.

Also in this place is the Altar of Incense where you become a pray-er and intercessor for others. As you sacrifice and travail for others, it is then that God meets with you in the Holy of Holies to commune in love and worship.

3) A Worshiper

Psalm 15 and Psalm 24 describe a worshiper who abides in the Tabernacle. The question is asked, "Who may abide in Your tabernacle?" or "Who may dwell in Your Holy Hill? The answers to these questions: "YOU".

By the grace of God, a true worshiper has clean hands and a pure heart. No works that you've done or words that you've said are enough to earn God's grace; it's all based on the precious works of Jesus Christ that you can stand as His tabernacle.

Remember, the word "tabernacle" means "dwelling place". Individually you are a dwelling place for God, but collectively, as the Body of Christ, we all grow into a holy Temple. This temple is made effective as we minister to God in the Outer and Inner courts and become even more powerful as we minister to others in our homes, jobs, and communities.

Ephesians 2:21-22

21) In whom the whole building, being fitted together, grows into a holy temple in the Lord,

22) In whom you also are being built together for a dwelling place of God in the Spirit.

A Worshiper in this New Tabernacle

"YOU", worshiper, are the tabernacle (temple) of God.

1 Corinthians 3:16

Do you not know that you are the temple of God and that the Spirit of God dwells in you?

Worshiper! God loves to be in your presence just as much as you want to be in His Presence! He loves you, and by singing these types of songs you maintain a tabernacle for God to dwell with you----He tabernacles with you, and you tabernacle with Him. This creates a beautiful relationship of love and fellowship! Amen!

CHAPTER 5

The Chosen Tribe

The tribe of Levi was hand-picked by God for specific duties and chosen to be near Him. What does this tribe in particular have to do with praise and worship? Look very carefully—this tribe was chosen by God because this tribe _chose God_. Exodus 32:36

Remember When?
Let's go back a little and remember when God called Moses up to the mountain for 40 days and 40 nights **(Exodus 24:12-18).**

Because of the long duration of time, the Children of Israel told Aaron to make gods for them because no one knew what happened to Moses. Of course, Aaron's leadership ability was not too tight that day and he paid attention to the people, and asked them to give up all their gold. As he was forming this so-called god in the fire, out popped this golden calf! To make a long story short, when Moses found out about it, he was so furious that he took the calf, threw it in the fire, ground it to powder and made the Children of Israel drink it.

I guess you could cut the anger and frustration with a knife. How did the Children of Israel come from worshiping the True and Living God to now being involved in worshiping a man-made golden calf? This was truly nothing but idol worship. But the defining moment comes when Moses makes this defining statement: "Whoever is on the LORD's side, come to me!"

Exodus 32:26 (NKJV)
"Then Moses stood in the entrance of the camp and said, 'Whoever is on the LORD's side—come to me!' And all the sons of Levi gathered themselves together to him."

This explains the very reason why the Tribe of Levi was the chosen tribe—this tribe chose God. Instead of choosing to engage in false worship, they chose to worship The God who delivered them from the hands of the enemy.

Have you chosen to take a stand for God? Have you chosen to be on His side and be a living sacrifice unto God; not being conformed to this world, but transformed by the renewing of your mind? This is as an act of your **spiritual worship**, and is acceptable and pleasing to God.

The Levites stood for righteousness by executing judgment on the people who had committed false worship. Rather than partaking in idolatry, they had a heart to worship God and God alone. And because of this, Moses says to them:

Exodus 32:29 (NIV)
"Then Moses said, 'You have been set apart to the LORD today, for you were against your own sons and brothers, and He has blessed you this day.'"

YOU ARE CHOSEN TO PROCLAIM HIS PRAISES!
Just as the Levites were chosen by God, you as a believer have been chosen to be a "royal priesthood" to "PROCLAIM THE PRAISES" of God!

1 Peter 2:9

But you are a chosen generation, a royal priesthood, a holy nation, His own special people, that you may proclaim the praises of Him who called you out of darkness into His marvelous light.

A FINAL NOTE TO REMEMBER

- Don't allow others to influence your worship.
- Don't allow a materialistic lifestyle take the place of God; "<u>always</u>" choose to worship God!

Historical Background
Of the Levites

Purposefully, I am going to be very extensive about our study of the Levites so that you can get a picture of how important this tribe was since they were chosen by God. The following is a snapshot of its origin:

Jacob had 12 sons; one of his son's names was Levi, henceforth came the Levitical tribe.

Genesis 35:23

23) Now the sons of Jacob were twelve: The sons of Leah were Reuben, Jacob's firstborn, and Simeon, LEVI, Judah, Issachar, and Zebulun;
24) The sons of Rachel were Joseph and Benjamin;
25) The sons of Bilhah, Rachel's maidservant, were Dan and Naphtali;
26) And the sons of Zilpah, Leah's maidservant, were Gad and Asher.

The Levites consisted of priests, prophetic musicians, singers, gate-keepers, doorkeepers, officers, judges, overseers, and treasurers.

Genesis 46:11 says that the sons of Levi were Gershon, Kohath, and Merari. From these three sons, the Levites were further separated into divisions. Numbers 3 gives us a census of the Levites and detailed information of their duties and positions in the tabernacle.

Breakdown of the (Levitical tribes)

Gershonites
Number: 7,500
Position in the Tabernacle: West, behind the Tabernacle
Duties: Maintenance of:
- The tabernacle
- The tent with its covering

- The screen for the door of the tabernacle
- The screen for the door of the court
- The hangings and their cords of the court

Kohathites
Number: 8,600
Position: South of the Tabernacle
Duties:
- Keeping in charge of the Sanctuary
- The Ark
- The Table
- The Lampstand
- The Altars
- The Utensils of the Sanctuary
- The Screen

Merarites
Number: 6,200
Position: North of the Tabernacle
Duties: Assembly and disassembly of:
- Boards of the tabernacle
- Bars, its pillars, its sockets
- Its utensils
- The pillars of the court, around with their sockets
- The pegs and their cords

Priests
Position: East of the Tabernacle
Moses, Aaron and his sons camped on the east of the tabernacle. Their duties were to keep charge of the sanctuary, and to meet the needs of the Children of Israel.

The sons of Aaron were additionally divided into 24 groups, each group responsible for temple sacrifices for 2 weeks each year. These men were set apart to sanctify the most holy things; they burned incense before the LORD to minister to Him, and to give the blessing in His name forever. (1 Chronicles 23:13).

The priests were to stand every morning to thank and praise the LORD, and likewise at evening, (1 Chronicles 23:30). As we ponder about our own personal devotions, is our thanksgiving and praise to God expressed in the morning and as we retire at night? Are we expressing thanksgiving as we represent Christ in our communities, on our jobs, and in our homes? Selah, let's pause and think of that.

When David was old and full of days, his census of the Levites from age 30 years and above was 38,000. (1 Chronicles 23:3)

24,000 - Looked after the house of the Lord
6,000 - Officers and judges
4,000 - Gatekeepers
4,000 – Musicians and singers

Encampment of the Tribes

The Bible says that many are called, and few are chosen, and it is clear to see that God chose the Nation of Israel to be a people close to Him. The encampment of the Tribes illustrates how the tribes were in position in relationship to the Tabernacle.

Twelve tribes were to surround the tabernacle; three tribes to the east; three tribes to the west, three tribes to the north, and three tribes to the south, (Numbers 2:1-31). Notice that the tribes positioned make the sign of the cross, which also points to Jesus.

Since the Tribe of Levi was positioned near the Tabernacle, they were not included in the actual 12-tribe encampment. Joseph's sons, Ephraim and Manasseh were adopted by Jacob and given the territorial inheritance, and are therefore included in the encampment. See Genesis 48:5-20. The example below explains the position of the tribes.

Twelve Tribes
12-1 (Levi) = 11
11-1 (Joseph) = 10
10+2 (Ephraim & Manasseh) = 12

North
Dan (62,700)
Asher (41,500)
Naphtali (53,400)

West	Levites			**East**
Ephraim (40,500)	Levites	Tabernacle	Priests	Judah (74,600)
Manasseh (32,200)		Levites		Issachar (54,400)
Benjamin (35,400)				Zebulun (57,400)

South
Reuben (46,500)
Simeon (59,300)
Gad (45,650)

The Marching Order of Praise

There is purpose and order in what God does, and the Bible expressly says, "Let all things be done decently and in order", I Corinthians 14:40. When God commanded the Israelites to travel in the wilderness, even their marching order had to be followed by instructions. I'm sure you're wondering why is this important and what does this have to do with praise; right? Well, let's find out.

First and foremost, God has momentum; He stays in motion. He knows each and everyone of us; where we've been, where we're at now, and where we're going. His desire is for us to keep up with Him, not Him keep up with us.

Very briefly we spoke about how the Children of Israel journeyed in the wilderness from one destination to the next; they visibly saw God's Presence take them from one place to the next.

<u>Numbers 9:17-18, 22, 23</u>
17) *Whenever the cloud was taken up from above the tabernacle, after that the children of Israel would journey; and in the place where the cloud settled, there the children of Israel would pitch their tents.*
18) *At the command of the LORD the children of Israel would journey, and at the command of the LORD they would camp; as long as the cloud stayed above the tabernacle they remained encamped.*
22) *Whether it was two days, a month, or a year that the cloud remained above the tabernacle, the children of Israel would remain encamped and not journey; but when it was taken up, they would journey.*
23) *At the command of the LORD they remained encamped, and at the command of the LORD they journeyed; they kept the charge of the LORD, at the command of the LORD by the hand of Moses.*

<u>Please note this important fact</u>: When it was time for the tribes to travel, the order of the march started with a portion of the tribe who

40

surrounded the tabernacle with praise; Why? They carried the Ark of the Covenant, which of course, signified the Presence of God. Remember, the Tribe of Levi were the only ones who could carry the Ark of the Covenant.

After the Ark of the Covenant, the first tribe that led the march was the Tribe of Judah. And guess what the name Judah means? PRAISE!!!! (Genesis 29:35). Do you think God is trying to tell us something?!!

As seen by the following example, the Levites marched in between each three (3) set of tribes. This example reflects the marching order of praise (Numbers 10:11-33).

Marching Order of the Tribes

God's Presence

⇑

*Levites carrying
the Ark of the Covenant*

⇑

March of the Tribe of Judah,
Issachar, Zebulun

*Levites carry
the Tabernacle*

⇑

March of the Tribe of Reuben,
Simeon, and Gad

⇑

*Levites carry
The Tabernacle furnishings*

⇑

March of the Tribe of Ephraim, Manasseh,
Benjamin

March of the Tribe of Dan, Asher,
Naphtali

This wonderful example illustrates that when God commands us to move, praise should be before us, behind us and in the middle of any and all situations of our lives.

Moses gave praises to God when the Ark set out to move, and also when it rested.

Numbers 10:35-36
35) "So it was, whenever the Ark set out, that Moses said: 'Rise up, O LORD! Let Your enemies be scattered, and let those who hate You flee before You'.
36) And when it rested, he said: 'Return, O LORD, to the many thousands of Israel'. "

As God is directing our everyday affairs and getting involved in our everyday lives, we can open our mouths and say, "Arise, LORD, and let Your enemies be scattered!" Psalms 68:1-5 expresses this praise:

Psalm 68:1-5
1) Let God arise, let His enemies be scattered; let those also who hate Him flee before Him.
2) As smoke is driven away, so drive them away; as wax melts before the fire, so let the wicked perish at the presence of God.
3) But let the righteous be glad; let them rejoice before God; yes, let them rejoice exceedingly.
4) Sing to God, sing praises to His name; extol Him who rides on the clouds, by His name YAH, and rejoice before Him.

What is the next move God has for you? Whatever you are told, the first thing out the gate should be praises to God!!

More Interesting Facts About
The Levites

THE LEVITES WERE NOT APPOINTED FOR WAR

In the first chapter of Numbers, the children of Israel had already been out of Egypt for about two years. At this point, God told Moses (who also came from the tribe of Levites, Exodus 6:20) to number all of the males, 20 years of age and upward for the purpose of war.

All the tribes were numbered EXCEPT for the Levites. Why? The Levites were not appointed for war, they were appointed for the service of the Tabernacle. I challenge you to do a study on this subject; however, in this particular passage, and as stated previously, the Levitical tribe was assigned to the setting up and taking down of the Tabernacle. No one could encamp by the Tabernacle except for the Levites. They were specifically set apart for the service of the Lord. Inasmuch, we as choir members are not for war, but for the service of the Lord! Amen!

THE LEVITES WERE APPOINTED BY GOD

Numbers 1:47-54.

47) "But the Levites were not numbered among them by their fathers' tribe;

48) For the LORD had spoken to Moses, saying:

49) 'Only the tribe of Levi you shall not number, nor take a census of them among the children of Israel;

50) But you shall appoint the Levites over the tabernacle of the Testimony, over all its furnishings, and over all things that belong to it; they shall carry the tabernacle and all its furnishings; they shall attend to it and camp around the tabernacle.

51) And when the tabernacle is to go forward, the Levites shall take it down; and when the tabernacle is to be set up, the Levites shall set it up. The outsider who comes near shall be put to death.

52) The children of Israel shall pitch their tents, everyone by his own camp, everyone by his own standard, according to their armies;

53) But <u>the Levites shall camp around the tabernacle</u> of the Testimony, that there may be no wrath on the congregation of the children of Israel; and the Levites shall keep charge of the tabernacle of the Testimony.'
54) Thus the children of Israel did; according to all that the LORD commanded Moses, so they did."

THE LEVITES WERE GIVEN TO AARON
Numbers 3:5

5) "And the LORD spoke to Moses, saying:
6) 'Bring the tribe of Levi near, and present them before Aaron the priest, that they may serve him.
7) And they shall attend to his needs and the needs of the whole congregation before the tabernacle of meeting. To do the work of the tabernacle.'"

THE LEVITES WERE A SUBSITUTE FOR THE FIRSTBORN
Originally every firstborn of the children of Israel were to be sanctified and set apart to God; however, the Levitical tribe was taken instead.

Numbers 3:12
12) Now behold, I Myself have taken the Levites from among the children of Israel instead of every firstborn who opens the womb among the children of Israel. Therefore the Levites shall be Mine.
13) Because all the firstborn are Mine. On the day that I struck all the firstborn in the land of Egypt, I sanctified to Myself all the firstborn in Israel, both man and beast. They shall be Mine: I am the LORD.

THE LEVITES WERE DEDICATED TO THE LORD
In Numbers 8:1-21, we see that the Levites were dedicated and ceremonially cleansed for the work of the Lord.

THE LEVITES SERVED FOR 25 YEARS
Numbers 8:23-25

23) "Then the LORD spoke to Moses, saying,

24) 'This is what pertains to the Levites: From twenty-five years old and above one may enter to perform service in the work of the tabernacle of meeting;

25) And at the age of fifty years they must cease performing this work, and shall work no more'."

THE LEVITES HAD NO INHERITANCE
The Levites received no inheritance when the children of Israel entered the promise land. Why? God provided for them through the tithes from the children of Israel. The Levites lived from the tithes in return for their work in the Tabernacle.

Numbers 18:21-24
Behold, I have given the children of Levi all the tithes in Israel as an inheritance in return for the work, which they perform, the work of the tabernacle of meeting.

THE LEVITES WERE GATEKEEPERS:
The gatekeepers were apparently third-class priest responsible for the care of the temple. This included a variety of tasks, such as guarding the entrance to the temple (1 Chron. 9:23-27; 2 Chron. 23:19), protecting the Ark (2 Chron. 15:23), and overseeing the collection and distribution of monetary offerings (2 Kings 12:9, 22:14; 2 Chron. 31:14). In our present churches, gatekeepers are called deacons and ushers.

THE LEVITES WERE APPOINTED TO CARRY THE ARK
1 Chronicles 15:2:

"Then David said, 'No one may carry the Ark of God but the Levites, for the LORD has chosen them to carry the Ark of God and to minister before Him forever'."

"Preaching to the Choir"

Did you know that choir members and musicians were first established in the Old Testament? Choir members and musicians were identified as "Levites", and it was commanded by King David that the Levites and priests surround the Ark of the Covenant with praise. Let's review the history of how it all began.

APPOINTED AS SINGERS
The Levitical tribe was appointed as singers by King David.

1 Chronicles 15:16 (NKJV)
Then David spoke to the leaders of the Levites to appoint their brethren to be the singers accompanied by instruments of music, stringed instruments, harps, and cymbals, by raising the voice with resounding joy.

Also, in scripture, King Solomon, appoints singers for the dedication of the house of God. Do you see what important roles singing and music are?

In 2 Chronicles 5:12-13, Solomon had completed the work for the house of the Lord, and the Levites, who were the singers, and the musicians who were trumpeters, harpists, violinist, etc., were as "one", to make "one" sound to be heard in praising and thanking the LORD.

Note: Choir members and musicians at that particular time were called "SINGERS".

I really want you to understand that you are not just someone singing songs in a choir; your position is much deeper than that. Notice once again (1 Chronicle 6:31-32) that David "Set over the service of song" to the Levitical tribe. Let's take another look – they "ministered" unto the Lord with singing. YOU ARE PLACED IN A CHOIR TO MINISTER!

You are a soloist to minister; a dancer to minister, and a musician to minister unto the Lord.

Sometimes we get focused with talent more than position, but we must re-evaluate our purpose and understand that our talent is to be used 100% for ministering.

PROPHETIC MUSICIANS AND SINGERS:
The Bible talks about the part of the Levites who were musicians that prophesied while playing their instruments, (1 Chronicles 25:1-7). Every musician should pause and think about what an important role you play in ushering in the Presence of God.

1 Chronicles 25:1
Moreover David and the captains of the army separated for the service some of the sons of Asaph, of Heman, and of Jeduthun, who should prophesy with harps, stringed instruments, and cymbals. And the number of the skilled men performing their service was:

1 Chronicles 25:7
So the number of them, with their brethren who were instructed in the songs of the LORD, all who were skillful, was two hundred and eighty-eight.

These prophetic musicians were musical composers and leaders of David's choir. Here's what the Bible says about some of their deeds.

II Chronicles 5:12
12) "And the Levites who were singers, all those of Asaph and Heman and Jeduthun, with their sons and their brethren stood at the east end of the altar, clothed in white linen, having cymbals, stringed instruments and harps, and with them one hundred and twenty priests sounding with trumpets—

13) indeed it came to pass, when the trumpeters and singers were as one, to make one sound to be heard in praising and thanking the LORD, and when they lifted up their voice with the trumpets and cymbals and instruments of music, and praised the LORD saying:

'For He is good, For His mercy endures forever,' that the house, the house of the LORD was filled with a cloud, so that the priests could not continue ministering because of the cloud, for the glory of the LORD filled the house of God.'"

Are you getting a clear picture of who the Levites were? They were set apart, dedicated, and sanctified by God to work near the tabernacle for the service of the Lord.

Quite interesting enough, we as choir members, and whoever are involved in praise and worship, should understand the importance of the service of the Lord. It is important that we are dedicated to God, and maintain a clean life as we prepare the congregation to enter into worship.

Even when we have rehearsals, we should be of one mind, one spirit, and one focus. This does not mean that we can't appreciate a diversity of ideas and opinions, but our main objective is to be in one accord for the purpose of ushering in the Presence of God.

THE LEVITCAL ASSIGNMENT

Have you ever thought about what a choir is suppose to do as we are engaging in praise and worship? King David also addresses this very question. As the Levites were chosen by God to carry the Ark, we as choir members have been chosen to carry God's presence into the Sanctuary.

1 Chronicles 16:4

And he appointed certain of the Levites to minister before the Ark of the Lord, and to record (commemorate), to thank, and to praise the LORD God of Israel.

David appoints certain Levites to minister, but this time he defines their office and roles by giving them an assignment:

1. To record (prayer and supplication)
2. To thank
3. To praise

The word record here means to invoke, which means to call on God for aid and protection; to address God in prayer and supplication. I like the way the amplified version describes it: to celebrate by calling to mind.

When we minister in the choir, are we singing songs that address Our Father in prayer and supplication? As a praise and worship leader, is the congregation enlightened with songs of celebration and do they call to mind the goodness of God? Are we reminding the congregation to give thanks? Is our expression one that points to God, and gives Him praise? As the Psalmist most adequately says, "Selah" – pause and think of that.

Psalm 22:3 says that God inhabits the praises of His people. Inhabit means to reside in, and occupy as a home. This also means that God is at home with our praise.

You see, David was creating an atmosphere where God could dwell. 1 Chronicles 16:6 says that the Levites and priests were "continually" before the Ark of the Covenant of God. Oh, what a place to be!

THE VALIDATION:

At this point, we see validation:
   ▪ Your POSITION: Praise Leader, Singer, Musician, Dancer

- Your PRESENCE: to invoke the Presence of God; to give thanks; to praise
- Your PURPOSE: to provide a habitation for God to dwell

Yes, you play an important part in the Body of Christ, but let's discuss the importance of the purpose and structure of the choir in today's society. Many think that as long as we can sing and play an instrument that this is all that is required, but I choose to believe that it goes a little deeper than that. The purpose of a choir is to have a heart of a worshiper and a heart of humility.

Organization of the Worship Ministry

Better is one day in your courts than a thousand elsewhere;
I would rather be a doorkeeper in the house of my God than dwell
in the tents of the wicked.
Psalm 84:10

Organization: God Supports Leadership & Authority
Many people believe that Psalm 84:10 was one of the Psalms of David; evidently, this scripture takes us back to Korah, who was a part of the tribe of Levi, in Numbers 16. There was a reason why the sons of Korah said that they would rather be a doorkeeper in the house of God; the reason being is that the heart of their forefathers was that of pride and rebellion against leadership that God had chosen (this leadership being Moses and Aaron). As a result of this rebellion, the earth literally opened its mouth and swallowed up Korah, his family, all cohorts and whatever belonged to them.

Subsequently many generations later, the "sons" of Korah quickly changed from a heart of rebellion to the heart of a worshiper, and through humility, they confessed that they would rather be a doorkeeper in the house of the Lord, than to dwell in the tents of wickedness; I believe they learned their lessons.

Does this remind you of someone? Yes, it does! It seems like Korah operated with the same pride as Lucifer, who was cast out of Heaven.

Doorkeeper; what is this about a doorkeeper? What does this have to do with the organization of worship?

POSITION OF A DOORKEEPER
- One who guards the entrance of the temple
- One who waits at the threshold to receive messages

Doorkeepers were also called gatekeepers or porters; *all are positions of humility*. Now hear what the Sons of Korah were saying.......my heart and my flesh cry out for the living God.........Blessed are those who dwell in Your house; they will still be praising You. Selah. The Sons of Korah found the secret to the heart of a worshiper, and that is to be at the entrance to God's Presence, praising God and waiting to receive from God.

By having the heart of a worshiper, each individual on the worship team must spend quality time waiting before the Presence of God; loving God, and pleasing the Father with a submitted life. Therefore, as we come together as one team and unit, we can prepare to carry His Presence by preparations of voice, skillful practice of dance, and instruments.

THE PURPOSE OF THE WORSHIP MINISTRY
The purpose of the Worship Ministry is not just singing and dancing, but most importantly, having a heart for God "first", and afterwards to skillfully and understandably reveal God's heart to the congregation through praise and worship. Having a heart for God prepares us to carry His Presence to the people.

1. Have the Heart of a Worshiper (Psalm 42:1-2)
    Have a yearning for God: Yearn = A strong desire or longing
2. Prepare to carry His Presence

Collectively we are the Worship Ministry, but individually, we are worshipers. Worshipers spend quality time with God 1 on 1, receiving God's heart. Consequently, just like the doorkeepers guarded the temple, we must guard our temples (body, mind, and soul) with the Word of God to be used of God. This will definitely prepare us for ministry.

With a heart of humility, we will prepare Him a habitation of praise and an atmosphere of worship! Amen!

Structure of the Worship Ministry

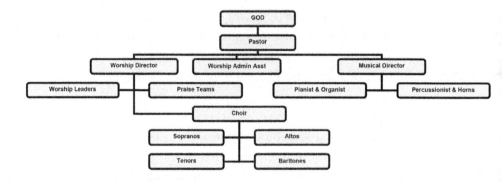

Organization: God Honors Structure

Organization existed since the beginning of time when God created the heavens and the earth. In unity and oneness, God, the Father; God, the Son; and God, Holy Spirit, worked together to bring order to an earth that was void and without form. _Just as God honors organization, we must honor the structure of the worship ministry._ The above organizational chart is only an example. Your ministry may be structured differently, however, please note that God's sovereignty is in charge.

Before Jesus performed the miracle of feeding the 5,000 He gave thanks and established order by making the people sit down in 50, then He gave the food to the disciples, and the disciples gave food to the multitudes.

Order is necessary to accomplish the purposes of God. This order is called: unity. There is an anointing in unity, Psalms 133:1

A unit or team cannot survive without structure and organization. A team or unit will only be as strong as its structure, and within that structure, certain elements must exist or it will collapse and be of none effect.

Elements that need to exist are simple, but much overlooked; these elements are:

- Love
- Vision
- Submission

Why are these things overlooked? Perhaps our concentration is based more on performance than relationship. Relationship with God and with one another takes preeminence to how well we minister or perform.

INTERESTING FACT:

- How I treat others affect my praise to God.
- How I treat my fellow choir members affect my worship to God.

LOVE

Though I speak with the tongues of men and of angels, but have not love, I have become sounding brass or a clanging cymbal.
1 Corinthians 13:1

In this very familiar love chapter, Paul says to us that even though we may speak the most eloquence of speech, if we have not love, our speech is a clanging cymbal. The Greek research on the words, "clanging cymbal" is to make a sorrowful, empty noise. With this in mind, though we can _sing_ with the most eloquent voice, if we have not love, our singing is pitiful and empty, and we are making noise rather than music.

We must understand that LOVE is the binding force that keeps us all together. LOVE is the central theme of the gospel, "For God so loved the world"...John 3:16, and hence, the motivation in all that we are must be centered on LOVE. Without love, our praise and worship is not effective, and guess what? If we do not love, then we do not know God.

1 John 4:8
He who does not love does not know God, for God is love.

Furthermore, our love must not only be expressed to God, but to one another, and this is truly expressing love in maturity.

1 John 4:11, 12
11) Beloved, if God so loved us, we also ought to love one another.
12) No one has seen God at any time. If we love one another, God abides in us, and His love has been perfected in us.

Referring back to the Love Chapter, 1 Corinthians 13:4-8 gives us a beautiful picture of what love is all about, as it is the model by which every Christian or choir member must live:

> *Love suffers long and is kind,*
> *Love does not envy,*
> *Love does not parade itself, is not puffed up;*
> *Loves does not behave rudely, does not seek its own.*
> *Love is not provoked, thinks no evil;*
> *Love does not rejoice in iniquity, but rejoices in the truth;*
> *Love bears all things, believes all things,*
> *Love hopes all things, endures all things*
> *Love never fails.*

VISION

> *Where there is no vision, the people perish:*
> *but he that keepeth the law, happy is he.*
> Proverbs 29:18 (KJV)

Vision is a necessary key to any corporation, and it expresses the mission to why a corporation exists. The Hebrew word "vision" means "sight" or "revelation", and the word "perish" means "to loosen or become less tight or firm". So where there is no sight or revelation, the worship ministry is not firm.

Under God's authority, the Pastor must carry out the vision he was given by God and express it to his directors, which in turn express vision to their teams. The importance is that everyone is working together for the same cause or vision to carry out God's will. To create cohesiveness, "love" and "vision" are interconnected throughout all levels, while "unity" is maintained by regulations and guidelines. Inasmuch, if we love God, we will abide by these principles set forth to enhance the Worship Ministry.

SUBMISSION
Submitting to one another in the fear of God
Ephesians 5:21

Many people cringe when they hear this word; as some think it carries the thought of weakness, but this is far from the truth. What is submission?

Submission – Greek word (hupotasso),
(hoop-ot-as-so) # G5293, G5259, G5021
- To be under the mission of another.
- To come under alignment to authority.

When we breakdown this word, it is defined as:
- Hupo – below, under or beneath
- Tasso – To arrange in an orderly manner or fashion

Hupotasso is a military word that means submission and surrender. It means to come under the authority of another; it means to arrange in military fashion under the commander; to dispose to a certain position; to determine, ordain or set in order.

Being submitted under authority is necessary because it teaches one how to operate in the Spirit by being in one accord. Power is released through submission as we are in sync with the Holy Spirit, with our pastors and worship leaders. We all are co-laborers with God as we yield to the promptings of the Holy Spirit and as we sing praises and worship God.

There is oneness and unity in Heaven's worship, and there should be oneness and unity upon this Earth through praise and worship; submission creates this oneness.

The next time you think of the word submission, imagine a submarine going under sea level on a mission. How does the submarine began its assignment?
- The submarine goes under water.
- The submarine is headed toward a destination
- The submarine has specific instructions to carry out

Sometimes a submarine can come under attack, but the equipment on board helps it to stay focused to carry its purpose. (Just like the Holy Spirit helps us to stay focused). The Worship Ministry is here to carry out a mission; what is it? To glorify God through praise & worship (even while under attack).

Let's be real, Worship Ministry! We are called to usher in the Presence of the Lord, and Satan is going to attack us because he wants his position back! He was kicked out of Heaven as the Worship Leader and we have taken his place as the Worship Ministry; do you think he's just going to sit back and do nothing? NO!!! So what we must do is stay on guard and submitted to God; resist the devil, and he will flee from us! Amen!

In conclusion, remember that in this submission, we are to honor organization:
- God reigns in sovereignty
- The Pastor submits to God's authority and vision
- The Worship Ministry Director submits to the Pastor's authority and vision
- The choir, band, and dancers submits to the Worship Director's authority
- And we all submit to one another in LOVE.

The Levitical Place

STANDING......
   at my post

CLEANSING......
   my vessel

READY.........
   to usher in the Presence of God

SINGING.........
   the High Praises of the King

WAITING.........
   for the Glory of God to fill the tabernacle

I'm standing in the Levitical Place!!!!

II Chronicles 29:17
......be not now negligent: for the Lord hath chosen you to STAND be-fore Him, to SERVE Him, and that ye should MINISTER unto Him......

CHAPTER **6**

Twelve Praises

Twelve is an interesting number; it represents government and order. There are many expressions of praise; however, I have discovered Twelve Praises that are powerful and can establish order in a worshiper's life.

The Halal Praise	The Yadah Praise
The Tehillah Praise	The Todah Praise
The Shabach Praise	The Taqa Praise
The Epainos Praise	The Karar Praise
The Tanah Praise	The Zamar Praise
The Barak Praise	The Zimrath Praise

As stated in the earlier chapter, praise is the expressed glorification of God; to honor God; to exalt and extol God. So whenever you hear someone say, "Praise the Lord", your response should be, "Yes, let's glorify and exalt the Lord."

The Bible is very simple and forthright in telling us that God is the central point of praise. Deuteronomy 10:21 says that "He is your God, and He is your praise." Another scripture, Jeremiah 17:14, says, "Heal me, and I will be healed. Save me, and I will be saved, for _You are my praise_." These scriptures definitely confirm that God is the central point of praise.

Purposes of Praise

The main purpose of praise is this: _To create an atmosphere where God can dwell._ You see, when we praise God, we are duplicating what is being done in Heaven, and we are setting up an atmosphere where God's power can be manifested to change lives, to heal, to deliver, and to save souls.

Again, the Bible says in Psalm 22:3 (KJV) that God inhabits the praises of His people. His power and anointing is present when we praise Him. His works are made manifest through praise. The Old King James Version uses the word, "inhabitest", which means reside or dwell, but the New King James Version states it this way:

"But You are holy; _enthroned_ in the praises of Israel".

What is this scripture saying? It is saying that God is holy, and God is enthroned as you praise Him.

Enthroned means:
1) To be on a throne; invested with power as a king.
2) To seat or place in a position of authority
3) To exalt; revere

Certainly we know that God is on the throne whether we praise Him or not; however, this means that as He is acknowledged on the throne and praised as the powerful, Almighty King, He is in position of authority to rule and reign in your life as He is exalted and reverenced.

This type of praise has nothing to do with how you feel, or what you think, or even who you are; but it has everything to do with who God is. The devil cannot participate in your life with this type of praise! You will completely stop him in his tracks and put him on lock down! This is "Alpha & Omega" praise---God will have the first word and He will have the last word in all your situations!

61

Evil has to go away from your surroundings when you use this praise. Proverbs 8:20 says: "A king who sits on the throne of judgment scatters all evil with his eyes." (NKJV). In the margin of my Bible, it states: "The discerning eye of a just king causes evildoing to be blown away like chaff." Isn't that wonderful?! God is going to blow away evil as a result of your praise! Hallelujah!!!

The Power of Praise Precedes God

What does this mean? Because God inhabits praise, praise should already be in the atmosphere before the manifestations of God. The Bible states in Psalm 65:1, "Praise is awaiting you, O God in Zion." This is the reason why we have praise and worship at the beginning of our church services---it sets the atmosphere.

The Purpose of Praise & Worship
- To glorify God.
- To honor and exalt God higher than the facts warrant.
- To create an atmosphere where God can dwell.

What are the Twelve Praises?

1. The Halal Praise – Praise of what the LORD has done; to praise; to laud; to shine; boast; rave, and to celebrate clamorously.

Strong's Concordance, #1984, Hebrew (Halal)
Pronounced, (haw-lal') – Psalm 150, Isaiah 12:2, Psalm 68:4

Extreme praise; to thank, rejoice, boast, and rave about God; to celebrate clamorously. Halal is the root from which the word "hallelujah" is formed. Hallelujah is the Hebrew word for "Praise the Lord". This phrase is not a suggestion, but a command: Hallelu-Jah (all of you must praise Jah). Jah , interpreted as **YAHH**, is the shorter version of the Lord's Holy Name, which is, **YAHWEH**, Strong's #H3050. It is also interpreted as Y'hovah (Ye-ho-vah), or Jehovah; Strong's #H3068, which means "**LORD**"; The Self-Existing, Eternal God.

Strong's #H3050, describes "**YAHH**" (pronounced "yaw") as **Jah; the Lord, Most Vehement**.

The following is a description of the word, vehement in which I believe describes **The Lord, Most Vehement**:

Aggressive	assertive	dynamic	energetic	forceful
full-blooded	muscular	resounding	strenuous	emphatic
vigorous	violent			

*Note: Emphasis on the word, "**full-blooded**":
- Containing fullness of substance
- Full of enthusiasm and energy
- Fully developed
- Genuine

This is certainly not the little baby Jesus, born in a manger, but the King of Kings, who is to return for His people! He is the King of Kings, and the Lord of Lords, who acts with great force, very fervent, <u>very ardent with affection</u>, passion, desire, eloquence, and power.

David experienced Jah, Jehovah, Yahweh in Psalms 18:6-19.

The driving force of **YAHH, Jehovah; The LORD, Most Vehement is LOVE**. Yes, it's because of His **LOVE** for you; His Bride, the Church whom He protects and cherishes that He is described in this manner. Jesus' love was demonstrated by the finished work of the Cross done at Calvary when He made a public spectacle of the devil. Colossians 2:15.

This is not YAHH, Jehovah, who is angry at you, but rather YAHH, Jehovah who is angry at the devil! For this is the reason and purpose why Jesus was manifested: that He might destroy the works of the devil! (1 John 3:8). He is a loving God who delivered you mightily from the hand of the enemy. Colossians 1:13-14

What Does Hallelujah Really Mean?

The following is a breakdown of the word: Hallelujah:

Halal - celebrate   *u* - you   *Jah* – YAHH/Yahweh or Jehovah = Hallelujah!

COMMAND:
- Praise the Lord!
- Hallelujah!
- Celebrate – you – Jah/YAHH - Jehovah/ Y'hovah
- Praise – you – YAHH
- Praise You Yahweh
- You shall praise God!

When "Hallelujah" is expressed upward, we are exalting and celebrating God. When we greet one another with the phrase, "Praise the Lord", or "Hallelujah", we are actually creating an atmosphere of celebration and success by reminding ourselves to **EXALT THE LORD** instead of magnifying our problems. Psalms 150:6 explains this so eloquently: Praise Him for <u>"His" mighty acts</u> and Praise Him according to <u>"His" Excellent Greatness</u>. Here's the command: Let everything that has breath praise the LORD! Amen!

PRAISE THE LORD - (GREEK)

Praise the Lord in the Greek is the word, "**Alleluia**", #G239, which means, "**An adoring exclamation!**, (Revelation 19:1-4). Whereas "Hallelujah" in Hebrew is a command, "**Alleluia**" in Greek is an <u>expression of love towards God</u> as you ascribe *salvation, glory, honor and power belonging to the Lord our God*! This adoration makes praise a little more personal as you love God for who He is. This expression also means, "**Alleluia**, *the LORD God Omnipotent reigns!* As expressed in **Revelation 19:6-7.**

Hallelujah truly is the highest praise! We must celebrate The King of Kings and The Lord of Lords for His sovereign rule forever-----Amen, Hallelu-JAH!!!

2. The Tehillah Praise – *A Praise "song" or "hymn"; a Psalm or song of celebration, or lauding of God, who is praise-worthy; the praise and exaltation of God; praises, songs of admiration.*

Strong's Concordance, #8416, Hebrew, (T'hillah)
Pronounced, (teh-hil-law'), (*tehillah*) - Psalm 100:4, Psalm 40:3

Also derived from halal is *tehillah*, or *tehillim* in the plural. The noun *tehillah* comes from the verb halal. The Hebrew title of the Book of Psalm is *Tehillim*, literally meaning <u>the Book of Praises</u>. The Book of Psalm was actually the Psalter or songbook for worship events in the temple in Jerusalem. They are suitable for prayer or recitation, but especially designed for singing; the Psalms provide the means for eager hearts to express their praises to Israel's Holy One.

The following are examples of Tehillah Praise:

- The Hallelujah Psalms
  - » Psalms 104-106; 111-113; 115-117
  - » Songs used in daily synagogue worship

- The Egyptian Hallel
  - » Psalms 113-118
  - » Songs used in connection with the Feasts of Passover, Feasts of Pentecost, and the Feasts of Tabernacles and dedications.

- The Great Hallel – Songs of Ascent
  - » Psalms 120-137
  - » The Songs of Ascent refer to 15 steps leading up to the temple and indicate that these songs were to be used in a liturgical procession up to the temple.

» This annual religious pilgrimage to Jerusalem brought the worshipers singing to Mount Zion.
» Read Isaiah 30:29.

3. The Shabach Praise – *A two-directional praise; the Shabach Praise is very special. This is a two-fold praise that does two things at one time.*
- A praise to loudly express the worthiness and approval of God; to express glory and joyfully celebrate the triumphal victory and honor of God.
- A praise that creates calmness and stillness within one's heart. It pacifies agitation within a worshiper's soul, giving the assurance that everything is going to be all right.

Strong's Concordance, #7623, #7624, Hebrew (Shabach), (Sh'bach)
Pronounced, (shaw-bakh'), (sheb-akh') - Psalm 149:6, Psalm 131:2

To commend, praise; to adore, to glory in God; to still, quiet, or pacify someone. *Shabach* goes in two directions, "praising", and "calming." The verb occurs 11 times in the Old Testament, eight (8) of which have to do with speaking words of praise. The other three (3) references speak either about calming or quieting things within one's heart.

A Praise of Worthiness
This is a radical praise that truly esteems and exalts God and His worthiness. This is a praise that involves your whole being as you clap, dance, wave your hands, and joyfully enjoy the presence of the Lord.

Psalm 95:1-3
1) OH come, let us sing to the LORD! Let us shout joyfully to the Rock of our salvation.
2) Let us come before His Presence with thanksgiving; let us shout joyfully to Him with Psalms.
3) For the LORD is the great God, and the great King above all gods.

Psalm 149:6-7

6) Let the high praises of God be in their mouth, and a two-edged sword in their hand,

7) to execute vengeance on the nations, and punishments on the peoples;

In today's terms, the familiar phrase is: *"When praises go up, blessings come down!"*

A Praise of Calmness

Have you ever been in a service where you were so hungry for the Presence of God that you didn't care who was listening? All you wanted to do was to express your thanksgiving and faith in praise to the Almighty God by lifting Him up; right? Do you remember how you felt after that praise? Yes, you were fully satisfied that you had been kissed by the Father; right?

The Shabach Praise not only touches God, but His touch is returned back to you. This is the two-fold blessing; once that praise comes back and blesses you, it brings calm and stillness to know that everything is all right.

Psalms 131:2

Surely I have calmed and quieted my soul, like a weaned child with his mother, like a weaned child is my soul within me.

Psalms 46:10

Be still, and know that I am God; I will be exalted among the nations, I will be exalted in the earth!

4. The Epainos Praise – Expresses praise for what God has done and recognition of who God is and His glory.

Strong's Concordance, #1868, Greek (Epainos)

Pronounced, (ep'-ahee-nos) – Psalm 126:1-3, Psalm 98:1-9, Ephesians 1:6

This is a praise of approbation and commendation; Epainos expresses not only praise for what God does for us, but also for who He is, recognizing His Glory.

Has there ever been a time in your life that you had to sit up and recognize that it was only God that did the work, and you couldn't get any credit for it? In Psalm 126, the Psalmist says that, "We were like those who dream; our mouth was filled with laughter; then they said, 'The LORD has done great things for us, and we are glad' ". This is Epainos Praise; praising God for what He has done, and recognizing His Glory!

Epainos Praise always points the praise back to God. Paul says in Ephesians 1:6, "To the praise of the glory of His grace, by which He made us accepted in the Beloved."

Joseph was an interpreter of dreams, but when Pharaoh acknowledged his gifting, Joseph pointed the praise back to God and said, "It is not in me; God will give Pharaoh an answer in peace." (Genesis 41:16).

Daniel was asked by King Nebuchadnezzar if he could interpret a dream, and Daniel responded, ".....there is a God in Heaven who reveals secrets, and He has made known to King Nebuchadnezzar what will be in the latter days." (Daniel 2:28).

Also noted in the Psalms:

Psalm 115:1
Not unto us, O LORD, not unto us, but to Your name give glory, because of Your mercy, because of Your truth.

Let us always remember that when praise comes to us, we must turn that praise around to give glory to God! Amen!

5. The Yadah Praise – *A praise of thanksgiving with extended hands or "lifting hands."*

PRAISE WITH "THE HANDS"
It is very appropriate for worshipers to lift their hands to the Lord while in a worship service. This is not only the proper thing to do; it is the Biblical thing to do. Praise with our hands is an expression of giving thanks to God. Worship with our hands is a little different than praise with our hands; this will be discussed in our worship chapter.

The following are two expressions of praise that deal with the "lifting" of our hands in "thanksgiving":

- Yadah Praise – Extended hands in thanksgiving for what is seen and manifested, praising God for what He has done, confessing who He is.
- Todah Praise – Extended hands in thanksgiving for what *has not* been seen or manifested; glorifying God for Who He is. This is a sacrifice of praise, and a praise of faith.

Yadah - Strong's Concordance #3034, #3029, Hebrew, (Yadah), (Y'da)
Pronounced, (yaw-daw'), (yed-aw') - Psalm 28:2 and Psalm 143:6

- To use (i.e., hold out) the hand
- To make confession
- To praise
- To give thanks, thankful, thanksgiving for what God has done.
- Yadah, the Hebrew word for "confess", derives from "yad", meaning an open or extended hand. The focus is on reaching to take hold of.
- Hands are also a symbol of power, strength, and dominion. Both opened and closed hands are powerful:
  » A closed hand or fist represents the power of debt/destruction, struggle or rebellion. When we have a closed hand,

we allow debt and destruction to have dominion over us.

» An opened hand represents the power of means/wealth and indicates reaching out to God, confessing His goodness. Inasmuch, the lifting of our hands to the Father also indicates God's dominion over us and that we are strengthened by God with wealth, not only monetarily, but in all aspects of life.

With Hands Extended:
- Yadah Praise involves confession of who God is and His faithfulness.
- Yadah Praise is to take a stand on what God says.
- Yadah Praise is to speak what is believed through faith and praise
- Yadah Praise is praise and thanksgiving for God's promises.

Yehudah (Judah) was so named when his mother declared, "Now will I praise [or thank] the LORD" (Genesis 29:35).

Daniel gave thanks when he was spared from the king's wrath (Daniel 2:23).

Solomon gives a true example of yadah praise in 2 Chronicles 6:12, 24-42.

6. The Todah Praise – *A Praise of Thanksgiving with extended hands; A sacrifice of praise*

Strong's Concordance, #8426, Hebrew (Todah)
Pronounced, (to-daw') – Psalm 42:5, 10, 11; Habakkuk 3:17-19

- An extension of the hand (lift up)
- An avowal or usually adoration
  » Avowal: affirmation, statement, confirmation, declaration, acknowledgement, admission, and confession

- A sacrifice of praise
- Specifically a choir of worshipers, Ezra 3:10
  » Scripture: Psalm 50:14, Psalm 42:5, 10, 11 and 2 Chronicles 20:21, Psalm 22:22

A Note to All Choir Members:

- It is truly a sacrifice to sing in a choir; it takes a lot of dedication and diligence, practicing one day a week, and ministering another day of the week. That is why a choir gives God, "Todah Praise" - because we are offering God a sacrifice to sing His praises.

The Bible says, "In everything give thanks, for this is the will of God in Christ Jesus concerning you", 1 Thessalonians 5:18. Yadah praise and Todah praise will help us to give thanks.

Since Yadah Praise is giving thanks with hands lifted for what is "seen" and already happened, Todah Praise is giving thanks with hands lifted for what is "not seen", or manifested. You may not see it, but praise God anyway! Both direct one to call on God with concentration on being joyful about having a right relationship with Him. The attention is focused on God not on our problems.

- **Todah praise** is truly a sacrifice of praise because you don't see the manifestation yet, but you continue to declare and affirm who God is.
- **Todah praise** is giving God a "**Yet Praise**" (Psalm 42:5, 10, 11) in particular Habakkuk 3:17-19
- **Todah praise** is a praise given in faith.

7. The Barak Praise – *A Praise of Blessing and Happiness*
Psalm 134:1-3, Psalm 145:1-2, Matthew 5:3-12

Have you ever heard of the phrase, "Bless the Lord"? This type of phrase is frequently used. There are many phrases and religious dialects that are too familiar with churches these days; however, sometimes these words are expressed mechanically and we forget what we're really saying or implying. As we educate ourselves to the meanings, we will tremendously benefit from the blessings.

The Bible commands us to lift up our hands and bless the Lord! Similar to Yadah and Todah praise, the Barak praise is also extending the hands to bless the LORD, and guess what? The blessing boomerangs into our lives to bless us again!

Psalm 134:1-3
1) Behold, bless the LORD, all you servants of the LORD, who by night stand in the house of the LORD!
2) Lift up your hands in the sanctuary, and bless the LORD.
3) The LORD who made Heaven and Earth bless you from Zion!

Strong's Concordance, Hebrew Definitions:
#H1288 - Barak - Pronounced, (baw-rak') –To kneel and bless God as an act of adoration
#H837 – Osher – Pronounced, (O'-sher) - Happiness; happy
Psalm 63:4; Psalm 103:1-5, Genesis 12:2, Matthew 5:3-12 (The Beatitudes), Proverbs 29:18

Strong's Concordance, Greek Definitions:
#G3107 – Makarios - Supremely blest; fortunate, well-off; happy
#G3106 – Makarizo – To call blessed; count happy, pronounce fortunate
#G2127 – Eulogeo – To speak well of; to invoke benediction upon; to prosper
#G2128 – Eulogetos – Adorable
#G1757 – Eneulogeo – To confer a benefit on
#G2129 – Eulogia - Reverential adoration; fine speaking, elegance of language, eulogy

72

As you can see, to bless God means to kneel in reverential adoration, and praise Him with elegance of speech; however, when we're blessed of God, we are happy, fortunate, and receive benefits. I believe this blessing is 4-directional:

- We bless the Lord
- The Lord blesses us
- We become a blessing
- We bless others

WE BLESS THE LORD:

- To extend the hand and acknowledge God as the only true source of greatness, sovereignty, and prosperity.
- To kneel and bless God as an act of adoration, and praise
- To speak well of God as a sign of respect.
- To congratulate (an applause), to thank, and to praise.
- To speak words of excellence

The Psalmist, David gives us a wonderful example of blessing the Lord:

Psalm 63:4
"Thus I will bless You while I live; I will lift up my hands in Your name".

In other words, David is expressing his way of life: blessing the Lord by lifting up his hands, confessing the Name of the Lord. What a beautiful example of how we can do the same, lifting our hands to God, confessing His Name as Jehovah Jireh, our Provider; Jehovah Nissi, our Victory, and Jehovah Shalom, our Peace. Amen!

TO BLESS THE LORD – A BENEFIT PACKAGE

Did you know that there are benefits received from blessing the Lord? Again, to bless the Lord is to extend the hand and speak well of Him; to single Him out as the one and only true God, Creator of Heaven and Earth, and to kneel before Him in acknowledgment of His greatness alone. However, when God blesses us, we receive the benefits of salvation, healing, preservation, favor, and so much more!

73

David makes these declarations:

Psalm 103:1-5

1) Bless the LORD, O my soul; and all that is within me, bless His holy name!

2) Bless the LORD, O my soul, and forget not all His benefits:

- Who forgives all your iniquities
- Who heals all your diseases
- Who redeems your life from destruction
- Who crowns you with lovingkindness and tender mercies
- Who satisfies your mouth with good things, so that your youth is renewed like the eagles

David not only proclaims that God loads us with benefits, but God escapes us from death!

Psalm 68:19-20

19) Blessed be the Lord, who daily loads us with benefits, the God of our salvation! Selah.

20) Our God is the God of salvation; and to God the Lord belong escapes from death.

Not only are we extending the hands in blessing God, but we also speak well of Him, in love and adoration. David is very personal in his expression of how much he loves the Lord:

Psalm 18:1-2

1) I will love You, O LORD, my strength.

2) The LORD is my rock and my fortress and my deliverer, my God, my strength, in whom I will trust: my shield and the horn of my salvation, my stronghold.

Again and again, David blesses the LORD:

Psalm 34:1

"I will bless the LORD at all times, His praise shall continually be in my mouth."

We can also use our words to bless the LORD in His greatness:

Jude 25

To the only wise God, our Savior, be glory and majesty, dominion and power, both now and forever. Amen.

Revelation 5:13

*"And every creature which is in heaven, and on the earth, and under the earth, and such as are in the sea, and all that are in them, I heard saying, '**Blessing**, and honor, and glory, and power, be unto Him that sits on the throne, and unto the Lamb forever and ever'!"*

THE LORD BLESSES US:
- To speak words invoking divine favor.
- The implication of speaking favor or prosperity upon one.

When God blesses us we receive the benefit of salvation, healing, preservation, protection, favor and so much more! For example, through grace, the LORD invokes blessings, divine favor, and prosperity upon Abram, and as a result, his life became very prosperous.

Genesis 12:2

I will make you a great nation; I will bless you and make your name great;

Genesis 13:2

Abram was very rich in livestock, in silver, and in gold.

God blesses Abraham with the benefit of having a son in his old age and to become a Father of many nations.

Genesis 17:5-6

5) "No longer shall your name be called Abram, but your name shall be Abraham; for I have made you a father of many nations.
6) "I will make you exceedingly fruitful; and I will make nations of you, and kings shall come from you."

BLESSING GOD DELIVERS ENEMIES INTO YOUR HANDS

Moreover, God blesses Abraham, through Melchizedek, and Abraham received the benefit of the blessing when God delivered enemies into his hand. Read Genesis 14:18-20

The Bible specifically tells us that the Lord will bless us as, His righteous people; and not only that, but His favor shall surround us.

Psalm 5:12

"For You, O LORD, will bless the righteous; with favor You will surround him as with a shield."

WE BECOME A BLESSING, - B'rakah, Strong's #1293
Pronounced (ber-aw-kaw)

When we become a blessing, it is called B'rakah. This means that we become prosperous, and liberal; we become a present to someone (as in a gift), and we become a pool to someone. We can interpret pool in two ways: being refreshing as a pool of water, or a pool of money, or a common fund to someone.

Whatever your interpretation, be certain of the fact that when God blesses you, His desire is that you bless others, Amen!

Extend the hand - BLESS OTHERS:
The Aaronic Blessing – Numbers 6:22-27

We can speak blessings on others to invoke the blessing of the Lord upon them. To bless others is to speak words of divine favor over them. The Aaronic Blessing is a prime example of this blessing. It is a Priestly Blessing that Aaron spoke over the Children of Israel, thereby invoking the Name of the Lord upon them.

We can speak these same blessings over our families:

May the LORD bless you and keep you;
May the LORD make His face shine upon you,
May He be gracious unto you
May the LORD lift up His countenance upon you
And give you peace.
Amen!

8. The Tanah Praise – *A praise of remembrance and rehearse; a praise of testimony.*

Strong's Concordance, #8567, Hebrew (Tanah)
Pronounced, (taw-naw') – Psalm 26:7, Judges 5:11
- To commemorate, to rehearse
- The idea of attributing honor
- To ascribe praise

Judges 5 – The Song of Deborah
Deborah, the only woman judge in Israel, wrote this entire chapter as a song ascribing praise, honor, and victory unto the Lord. She is rehearsing and commemorating and giving a testimony of God's miraculous works not only in her time, but also how God previously brought the Children of Israel out of the wilderness.

Remember when God did something for you and the overwhelming excitement made you want to tell the whole world? This is the time to give God Tanah Praise—a praise of telling the goodness of God and all that He has done for you!!!! It's a praise to remember and rehearse all the victories He's brought you through!!!

Amen!!!

9. The Taqa Praise – *Clap Your Hands* – *A Praise of Victory*

Strong's Concordance, #8628, Hebrew (Taqa)
Pronounced, (taw-kah') - Psalm 47:1-9
- To slap the hands together
- To clatter
- To clang (with an instrument)

The Taqa Praise indicates energy and enthusiasm. In this Psalm, all nations are commanded to clap their hands to the triumphant King over all the earth. He is most awesome! This clapping and shouting is an indication of victory.

This praise is similar to the excitement of when someone makes a basketball point or touchdown at a football game at the last minute of the game! Of course, your first impression is to clap your hands.

Jesus gained victory over the devil – Clap your hands! **Psalms 98:1**

10. The Karar Praise – *Dance Before the Lord* – *A Praise of Victory*

Strong's Concordance, #3769, Hebrew (Karar)
Pronounced, (kaw-rar') – Psalm 150:4, 2 Samuel 6:14
- To dance
- To whirl

2 Samuel 6:14-23, Exodus 15:20-21
David danced before the Lord with all his might. This was also an indication of victory, as David was thoroughly excited about bringing back the Ark of the Covenant into the House of Israel.

King David gives us a wonderful description of dance:

2 Samuel 6:14
"Then David danced before the LORD with all his might; and David was wearing a linen ephod."

2 Samuel 6:12-21
Verse 12 -, David is bringing the Ark of the Covenant to his house with "gladness".

Verse 14 - This gladness turned into "dancing before the LORD with all his might.

Verse 16 – David was leaping and whirling. It literally means that he was spinning around, so much so that Michal, Saul's daughter, says that he was "uncovering" himself. What David was actually doing was dancing so much that his kingly robe fell off of him, but he continued to wear the linen ephod, which is the apparel of the priests.

Verse 20 – After being accused of uncovering himself shamelessly before the maidens (by Michal), King David's response to her was this:

Verse 21: "IT WAS BEFORE THE LORD".
What can we learn from David?
1. We should be "glad" about the Presence of God.
2. Our expression of dancing is appropriate in His Presence.
3. Our expression of dancing should be with all our might (not mediocre).
4. Dancing should be expressed spiritually, not sensually.
5. DANCE BEFORE THE LORD, not men.

PRAISE WITH MUSICAL INSTRUMENTS AND VOICES

*11. The **Zamar Praise** – Voice and Music*

Strong's Concordance, #2167, Hebrew (Zamar)
Pronounced (zaw-mar') – Psalm 149:3
- To Sing with voices and musical instruments
- To strike with fingers
- To touch the string or parts of a musical instrument
- To make music, accompanied by the voice
- To celebrate in song and music
- To give praise, sing forth praises, and psalms.

MUSICAL INSTRUMENTS & CHOIR
Musical instruments are an integral part of praise and worship. King David exemplified this through the majority of his reign. **2 Chronicles 5:12-14**

*12. The **Zimrath Praise** – Music only*

Strong's Concordance, #2176, Hebrew (Zimrath)
Pronounced (zim-rawth') – 1 Samuel 16:23
- To play music instrumental.

When Saul was under a distressing spirit, King David played an instrumental, and Saul was refreshed.

1 Samuel 16:23
And so it was, whenever the spirit from God was upon Saul, that David would take a harp and play it with his hand. Then Saul would become refreshed and well, and the distressing spirit would depart from him.

In conclusion, this is how we should praise the Lord:

- With "joyfulness"
- Serve the LORD with "gladness"
- Come before His Presence with "singing"
- Enter into His gates with "thanksgiving"
- Enter into His courts with "praise"
- Make His praise glorious (Psalm 66:2)
- Lifting our hands (Psalm 134:2)
- Clapping our hands (Psalm 47:1)
- Praise Him with the timbrel and dance (Psalm 150:4)

Raise the Praise

(A Summary of Praise)

Type of Praise	Definition
The Tehillah Praise	A Praise song or hymn of the mighty deliverances of God, singing and exalting God; songs of admiration Psalm 100:4, Psalm 40:3
The Epainos Praise	A Praise of what God has done, recognizing His Glory Psalm 98:1-9, Ephesians 1:6
The Halal Praise	A Praise of Celebration • A command to praise the Lord! • Hallelujah: Celebrate You JAH Psalm 150, Psalm 68:4, Isaiah 12:1
The Shabach Praise	A Praise of Worthiness A Praise of Calmness • When praises go up, blessings come down! Psalm 149:6, Psalm 131:2
The Yadah Praise	A Praise of Thanksgiving • Lifting hands to God of what is seen Psalm 28:2, Psalm 143:6
The Todah Praise	A Praise of Thanksgiving • Lifting hands to God of what is "not" seen • A Sacrifice of Praise Psalm 42:5, 10-11; Habakkuk 3:17-19
PRAISE HIM!	

Raise the Praise

(A Summary of Praise)

Type of Praise	Definition
The Barak Praise	A Praise of Blessing and Happiness • Lifting our hands to Bless God • God Blesses Us • We Become a Blessing • Extend the hands to bless others Psalm 134:1-3, Psalm 145:1-2, Matthew 5:3-12
The Tanah Praise	A Praise of Testimony • Telling of the goodness of the Lord Psalm 26:7
The Taqa Praise	A Praise of Victory • Clapping the hands as a sign of victory Psalm 47:1-9
The Karar Praise	A Praise of Victory • Dancing before the Lord as a sign of victory Psalm 150:4, and 2 Samuel 6:14
The Zamar Praise	A Praise of Voice & Music Psalm 149:3
The Zimrath Praise	A Praise of Music Only 1 Samuel 16:23
PRAISE HIM!	

Preaching to the Choir
Part 1

The Bible says that God gives us the garment of praise for the spirit of heaviness, Isaiah 61:3. As choir members, we must remember to put on the garment of praise before ministry to the congregation. Let's face it; sometimes we are not in the best of moods, but by putting on the garment of praise by spending quality "Praise-Time" before the Lord will cast off the oppressive works of darkness.

David says in Psalm 34:1 – "I will bless the LORD at all times; His *praises* shall continually be in my mouth." How can David have this expression of praise continually? Answer: He is blessing the Lord and the Lord's praises are in his mouth, in contrast to David's problems being in his mouth.

The following are question and answers to further inspire and build your faith as you praise the Lord! Amen!

- **What are the effects of praise?**
Praise CHANGES our environment (Acts 16:25-27)
Praise DISTRACTS the enemy and ushers in victory and power (2 Chronicles 20:22)
Praise silences the devil (Psalm 8:2)

- **Why praise?**
Because praise is pleasant - Psalm 147:1 - *Praise ye the Lord; for it is good to sing praises unto our God, it is pleasant, and praise is comely* (KJV).

- **What do you praise God for?**
There are plenty of reasons what to praise God for; it would take too many pages to list them, but here are a few:
    - First and foremost, for salvation (Revelation 19:1)

- His mighty acts, and according to His Excellent Greatness (Psalm 150:2)
- For His merciful kindness (Psalm 117:2)
- For His counsel (Psalm 16:7)
- For His help (Psalm 42:5, Psalm 46:1)
- Put on the garment of praise for the spirit of heaviness (Isaiah 61:3)

I'm sure you can personally think of many reasons to praise God. When you think about His goodness, you've just got to <u>PRAISE HIM</u>!

- **<u>TAKING IT TO A HIGHER LEVEL</u>**

When God created the heavens and the earth, it was the Holy Spirit who moved upon the earth and began to bring into form the things that were spoken by God. This is what the Bible says:

Genesis 1:2b
And the Spirit of God was hovering over the face of the waters.

The word hovering means a sweeping or moving, and it is this same Spirit that is hovering over you today. Have you ever thought about taking your praise to the highest level of expression? You cannot do this on your own; you need the help of the Holy Spirit to do this. As the Bible says, the Holy Spirit is our Helper; it is His job to do what we can't do. The satisfaction of taking your praise to a higher level depends on the Holy Spirit. When we read the Old Testament, many times you read statements like, "The Spirit of the Lord is upon me." In fact, Jesus spoke those same words in Luke 4:18.

Luke 4:18-19
18) The Spirit of the LORD is upon Me, because He has anointed Me to preach the gospel to the poor; He has sent Me to heal the

brokenhearted, to proclaim liberty to the captives and recovery of
sight to the blind, to set at liberty those who are oppressed;
19) to proclaim the acceptable year of the LORD.

The Prophet Ezekiel was also helped by the Holy Spirit in his ministry.

Ezekiel 43:5
The Spirit lifted me up and brought me into the inner court; and behold, the glory of the LORD filled the temple.

Without the Holy Spirit; we can't pray, we can't sing, we can't witness, and we can't do anything! After Jesus was filled with the Holy
Spirit, He began to minister. In conclusion, we need the Holy Spirit
to help us PRAISE GOD!

I Corinthians 14:15 says:
What is the conclusion then? I will pray with the spirit, and I will also
pray with understanding. I will sing with the spirit and I will also sing
with understanding.

What does it mean to sing with the spirit, and sing with understanding?

With the assistance of the Holy Spirit, it is actually _your spirit_ singing
with grace and making melody in your heart to the Lord. This is done
through singing Psalms, hymns, and spiritual songs.

Question: How are we to sing spiritual songs?
Answer: Let the word of Christ dwell in you.

Colossians 3:16
Let the word of Christ dwell in you richly in all wisdom, teaching and
admonishing one another in psalms and hymns, singing with grace in
your hearts to the Lord.

When you read and meditate on the Word of God every day, it is going to cause Christ to dwell in you, and the Holy Spirit is going to confirm the Word in you by speaking and singing.

The Bible encourages us to speak psalms and sing spiritual songs to one another and to the Lord.

Ephesians 5:18-19:
And do not be drunk with wine, in which is dissipation, but be filled with the Spirit, speaking to one another in psalms and hymns and spiritual songs, singing and making melody in your heart to the Lord.

Of course, those of you who partake singing with the Spirit in unknown tongues <u>during your private personal expressions</u>, will also be singing about the wonderful works of God, similar to when the Holy Spirit was given to the Apostles (Acts 2:1-11).

Prayer

Heavenly Father,

Thank you for this precious gift of singing in the Spirit. May this gift draw us closer to You through singing with grace, and making melodies in our hearts, and more than anything, let Your Presence be glorified through praise and worship to the fullest measure.

In Jesus' Name
Amen.

- ### Sing Praises with Understanding
The Bible specifically says that we should sing praises with understanding. This is a little different than the aforementioned singing with the spirit and singing with understanding. The difference is that we

are adding skillful knowledge of voice and music with the knowledge of knowing and understanding God.

Psalm 47:7
For God is the King of all the earth; sing praises with understanding.

What does it mean to sing praises with <u>understanding</u>?

<u>Understanding (Hebrew, #7919) – (sakal)</u>
Pronounced (saw-kal)

"Un<u>derstanding</u>" tell us how to sing:

- <u>Intelligently</u> – To be circumspect (to take heed)

This deals with understanding what or to Whom we're singing about

- <u>Skillfully</u> – To consider, to be an expert, to instruct, to teach
  » Spiritual and vocal instruction

- <u>Successfully</u> – To have good success, make to understand with wisdom so that your praise is effective and purposeful.
  » Spiritual and vocal instruction

Psalm 47:2
For the Lord Most High is awesome; He is a great King over all the earth.

Since God is a great King, He deserves honor and praise from His people. He deserves the highest respect that we can give Him.

When you <u>understand</u> that He is a great King over all the earth, you can praise Him!

When you <u>understand</u> that He is Jehovah-Tsidkenu, the Lord God your righteousness, you can praise Him!

When you <u>understand</u> that He is Jehovah-Rapha, the Lord God that heals you, you can praise Him!

When you <u>understand</u> that He is Jehovah-Nissi, the Lord God your victory, you can praise Him!

Should I say more?

- **<u>Sing Praises with Faith</u>**

The Bible says it is impossible to please God without faith, and it is impossible to *praise* God without faith. Our praise goes hand in hand with our faith. As we believe God's word, we allow the Holy Spirit to fill our minds with faith, and this causes us to dance and sing before the Lord our God.

In 2 Chronicles 20, Jehoshaphat was in trouble, in fact, the Bible says, "a great multitude is coming against you." Have you ever had anyone against you? Well, we see here in this chapter that Jehoshaphat did these things:

1. He set himself to seek the LORD.
2. He proclaimed a fast.
3. He began to ask help from the LORD.
4. He began to pray and worship by telling God who He is.
5. He reminded God of His mighty acts of the past.
6. He reminded God of His Word.

King Jehoshaphat was actually setting himself up for victory. One of the last things that he did was this:

2 Chronicles 20:21-22
"And when he had consulted with the people, he appointed those who should sing to the LORD, and who should praise the beauty of holiness, as they went out before the army and were saying:

'Praise the LORD
For His mercy endures forever!'"

Now when they began *to sing* and *to praise*, the LORD set ambushes against the people of Ammon, Moab, and Mount Seir, who had come against Judah; and they were defeated.

This is a true example of praising God in faith, because Jehoshaphat was expecting God to fight for them, and by this expectation (faith), his enemy was defeated. Praise God!

- **ANOTHER EXAMPLE OF PRAISE**
Another example of the expression of singing with faith in God is found in Acts 16:22-40, in particular, verses 25 and 26.

25) But at midnight Paul and Silas were praying and singing hymns to God, and the prisoners were listening to them.
26) Suddenly there was a great earthquake, so that the foundations of the prison were shaken, and immediately all the doors were opened and everyone's chains were loosed.

Paul and Silas weren't singing just so that the prison doors could be opened; they were singing because they loved God and out of dedication to Him. They rejoiced through suffering. And because of this, the Lord caused an earthquake which loosed everyone's chains. ALL doors were opened and ALL chains were loosed—a natural catastrophe responded to a spiritual phenomenon! Not only that, but salvation came to the keeper of the prison and he and his entire household believed on the Lord.

Praise God!

Q: What will you do when faced with persecution and imprisonment?
A: Sing Praises!

Q: What will you do when imprisoned with thoughts of oppression?
A: Sing Praises!

Q: What will you do when imprisoned with thoughts of suicide?
A: Sing Praises!

Q: What will you do when imprisoned with thoughts of lack?
A: Sing Praises!

Q: What will you do when imprisoned with thoughts of defeat?
A: Sing Praises!

Q: What will you do when imprisoned with thoughts of sickness and disease?
A: Sing Praises!

God will inhabit your praise and the foundations of your life will change!

Oh! Sing Praises!

Point Your Problems to His Presence

What happens when there are seasons of devastation in your life and you're too heavy in spirit to sing praises? The Book of Job tells us what to do: **_WORSHIP_**, Job 1:20. You might need to remain in a time of worship to allow God to heal your wounds. Eventually this worship will spring forth into praises for what God will do in regards to the situation. The weight of the matter is whether you praise or worship, point your problems to His Presence!

Preaching to the Choir
Part 2

A Heart Condition: Praises From the Heart

There are key ingredients that should not only be in a Christian's lifestyle, but most importantly, _must be_ evident in a choir member, soloist, or musician's life as well. These ingredients will allow you to be a conduit through which God can freely use you to minister unto the Lord and unto the people.

Two key ingredients that make up this flavorful masterpiece are:
- The condition of our hearts
- Our character

Both have a lot to do with the effectiveness of our praise. Let's look at what God says:

Isaiah 29:13
"Therefore the Lord said:

'Inasmuch as these people draw near with their mouths and honor me with their lips, but have removed their hearts far from Me. And their fear (reverence) toward Me is taught by the commandment of men.'"

This scripture is saying that we are giving God lip service, and our hearts are far from Him, and our reverence toward Him is being taught by men, instead of God.

We cannot emphasize enough that our hearts must be purposeful in our praise to God.

Psalm 9:1 – *I will praise thee, O LORD with <u>my whole heart</u>; I will show forth all thy marvelous works.*

Psalm 57:7 – *<u>My heart is fixed</u>, O God, my heart is fixed: I will sing and give praise.*

Psalm 108:1 – *O God, <u>my heart is fixed</u>; I will sing and give praise, even with glory.*
> Note: Fixed means steadfast; steadfast means
> Not changing; not moving, firm in purpose.

God does not like half-heartedness. There is no mediocrity in God. You're either for Him or against Him. You're either hot or cold, or He'll vomit you out of His mouth. That doesn't sound nice, but that is what the Bible says in Revelation 3:16. Therefore, when we come to praise and worship, God needs your "<u>whole heart</u>".

How can we sing effectively and praise God when our hearts are hurting, and we have strife, jealousy, competition, unforgiveness, and hatred on the inside of us? How can we sing and give praise to God, and at the same time have adultery in our hearts? Can we sing and praise God and not walk in love? <u>THE ANSWER IS "NO, WE CAN'T DO IT!"</u> When you're in the choir, standing before God with your beautiful clothes, and uplifted hands, the only thing that God is interested in is your <u>HEART</u>.

If we have these types of issues in our heart, God would rather deal with the issues first, so that we can have a whole-hearted worship later.

In John 4:19-24, the Samaritan woman at the well gives us a prime example of how most of us view worship. Her idea of worshipping God was superficial, as her emphasis was more external than internal.

John 4:20

"Our fathers worshiped on this mountain and you Jews say that Jerusalem is the place where one ought to worship."

Her dialect with Jesus communicates to Him that she is more concerned about the place to worship, yet Jesus showed her the way. He says that true worshipers that God seek are those who worship in spirit and truth. He was letting her know that the place was irrelevant, but the real worship must come from within. Your spirit (heart) must be centered toward God. You must be true to Him, and to your fellow man.

We must ask for God's help in revealing to us what is right and wrong through the mirror of His Word, and of course through confessing our sins. This is a cleansing process. God is not interested in our selfish motives. He is more interested in our heart and character. What issues are you dealing with? Can you give God your deepest secrets, and most painful heart? He can and will heal you, even at this very moment.

Psalm 15 gives us an example of a person with character. This is a standard we all should live up to; it is certainly not to condemn us, but to improve us. I refer to this scripture as a self-evaluation of the lifestyle of a worshiper, and often revert back to it when I feel myself being "un-Christian-like".

David asked these questions: LORD, who shall abide in Thy tabernacle? Who shall dwell in Thy holy hill? The answer is this:

1. He that walks uprightly.
2. He that works righteousness.
3. He that speaks the truth in his heart.
4. He doesn't backbite.
5. No evil to your neighbor.

6. He despises a vile person, but honors a righteous person.
7. He keeps his word and doesn't change it, even if it hurts.
8. He doesn't charge interest on money.
9. He doesn't take a reward against the innocent.

Once again, this is certainly not condemnation, but it is to help us come up to the standard of righteous living so that God's presence can have no hesitancy, but freely flow through us as we sing and minister to others.

The way we treat one another, affects our praise and worship to God. The Bible says that if we have an aught against our brother, we should leave our gift at the altar, and make things right. This scripture is actually talking about prayer, but it applies to praise also. Our praise must be pure before God, and when we have something against our brother, this will not allow our praise to be pure. Before you minister unto the Lord, take a moment to forgive and love, and watch how God's presence comes upon you!

The Three "R-Factors"

There are certain factors that should exist in a praise singer/musician, and worship leader. These factors are essential for maintaining a life-style of praise and worship in which I call, The Three "R-Factors":

- Relationship
- Reverence
- Refreshing

RELATIONSHIP: (Love for God)

A choir member must have a relationship with God through Jesus Christ our Lord. Upon having this relationship, it must be based upon your love for God, your obedience to God, and pursuing the will of God in your life. How is your love-walk with God? Do you treasure the time when you can get up in the morning and begin your day with a song of praise and prayer? When you lay down at night, is there a word of thanks for what the Lord has done for you through the day? (1 Chronicles 23:30)

God should have preeminence in our lives, and He should be our first love, as this is so beautifully quoted in the Bible:

Mark 12:30

"And you shall love the LORD your God with all your heart, with all your soul, with all your mind, and with all your strength. This is the first commandment."

God is due to receive our love, because He so affectionately loved us FIRST, as stated in John 3:16. And because of this, we should express love to Him every day! Expressing love to God is pure worship.

RELATIONSHIP: (Love for the Word)

A praise singer must maintain a love for God's Word on a daily basis. When there is maintenance of God's Word, you are able to minister unto people freely. As you invest spending quality time in the Word, the Holy Spirit will bring the remembrance of the Word back to you as you minister unto the people. David said,"Thy Word have I hidden in my heart that I might not sin against Thee." The Word will flow through you because the Word is in you.

In John 15, our Lord refers to Himself as the Vine, God the Husbandman, and we are the branches. He goes on to say that, "For without Me, you can do nothing."

John 15: 4-5
4) "Abide in Me, and I in you. As the branch cannot bear fruit of itself, unless it abides in the vine, neither can you, unless you abide in Me. 5) I am the vine, you are the branches. He who abides in Me, and I in him, bears much fruit; for without Me you can do nothing."

We cannot sing effectively without Him. Yes, we can use our talent and sing beautifully and capture every note like a bird, but are we allowing the congregation to experience a closer walk with Jesus? Are we speaking to their heart in song, so that the Holy Spirit can convict them of their sins and bring them to Jesus? Are we singing to the congregation whereas to bend them toward God in worship? Selah... pause and think of that.

RELATIONSHIP: (Love for your Fellowman)
As previously stated, we are commanded to love the Lord our God with all our heart, all our soul, all our mind, and all our strength and we are also commanded to love our neighbors.

Mark 12:31
"And the second, like it, is this: 'You shall love your neighbor as yourself.' There is no other commandment greater than these."

Real love is this: First Corinthians chapter 13. We know the chapter very well, but are we practicing what we preach? It's easier said than done. You may wonder what difference does this mean to a singer. The answer is, "everything."

When we do not operate in love, but walk in the flesh with envy, strife, and contentions, and have no check in our own love-walk, what kind of message are we sending? We are human, and we flare up sometimes, but we must be like David and say this prayer: "Create in me a clean heart, O God, and renew the right spirit within me."

Other scriptures to ponder are:

John 13:34-35
34) "A new commandment I give to you, that you love one another; as I have loved you, that you also love one another.
35) By this all will know that you are My disciples, if you have love for one another."

John 15:12
"This is My commandment, that you love one another as I have loved you."

Romans 13:8-10
8) "Owe no one anything except to love one another, for he who loves another has fulfilled the law.
9) For the commandments, 'You shall not commit adultery,' 'You shall not murder,' 'You shall not steal,' 'You shall not bear false witness,' 'You shall not covet,' and if there is any other commandment, are all summed up in this saying, namely, 'You shall love your neighbor as yourself.'
10) Love does no harm to a neighbor; therefore love is the fulfillment of the law."

REVERENCE:
By reverence, I'm referring to a heart that acknowledges God as holy: being truthful to God and walking in integrity and respect before God and man.

This was mentioned previously, but whatever position you hold in praise and worship, there must be order in your reverence and submission:

1. To God.
2. To the Pastor.
3. To the Worship Pastor or Minister of Music.
4. To the Praise and Worship Leader.
5. To the Directors.
6. To the Musicians.
7. To Choir members.

In general, as Christians, we must submit to God, and be submitted to one another. Jesus operated in submission by listening to God, and doing whatever the Father asked of Him, and Jesus, being all God and man, submitted to His parent's authority, yet He knew He had to be about His Father's business.

Other examples of reverence and submission: Joshua was submitted under Moses; Elisha was submitted under Elijah. David was submitted under Saul (until Saul's death). All of these men were anointed and under authority.

REFRESHING:
In addition to ushering the Presence of the Lord into the sanctuary, our next objective should be that of refreshing the congregation through what has taken place. The congregation's thought should not be, "Wow! That was a great show!" The truth of the matter is, the congregation should be saying, "I have been brought into the Presence of God."

In 1 Samuel 16:14-23 King Saul was overtaken by an evil spirit because of his disobedience. They told Saul that they would find a musician to play for him. (Let all the musicians say amen!) This musician happened to be David, and yes, David was a musician before he became King. Please pay close attention to verse 23:

1 Samuel 16:23

"And so it was, whenever the spirit from God was upon Saul, that David would take a harp and play it with his hand. Then Saul would become refreshed and well, and the distressing spirit would depart from him."

Think about this: David played for Saul, and his playing refreshed Saul. Let this thought really reside deep into your inner most being… David's playing refreshed Saul, and made him feel better. His playing brought relief to Saul. Let us as musicians and singers know that our playing and singing can also bring healing, freedom from depression, and deliverance.

As we prepare our hearts to minister to the congregation through the selection of songs, let us first ask ourselves: Is my life refreshed through my own praise and worship to God? Will the congregation be refreshed, through the musical instruments and my song of praise? And most importantly, is God pleased?

Paul mentions this about Philemon:

Philemon 1:7

"For we have great joy and consolation in your love, because the hearts of the saints have been refreshed by you, brother."

Philemon 1:20

"Yes, brother, let me have joy from you in the Lord; refresh my heart in the Lord."

As we take a closer look, we can see particular elements that accompany refreshing: GREAT JOY, CONSOLATION, and LOVE. These elements should also be present in us as we conduct our praise and worship services.

Paul also says in 1 Corinthians 16:18

For they refreshed my spirit and yours. Therefore acknowledge such men.

This scripture is referring to men who supported Paul's ministry, but we can also keep in mind how we can refresh our pastor and others by supporting their ministries.

Here are additional scriptures about refreshing to meditate on:
Romans 15:32
2 Corinthians 7:13
2 Timothy 1:16

CHAPTER 7

The Worship

Worship at the beginning of church service is wonderful. Worship in our own personal devotional time is very satisfying; however, we've been conditioned too long to think that worship ends at this point. Yes, singing the praises of our Father is heartfelt; yes, lifting our hands in adoration to the Lord can be sincere; and hearing musical renditions of worship is enjoyable, but Satan would rather us stop right there than to go any further. Moreover, once you experience worship on a deeper level, you will begin to find the treasures of God's will for your life.

As there are various types of praise, so are there various types of worship. The following are just a few ways that we can express worship to God.

Please note that "idol worship" is listed to denote the contrast between true worship and false worship.
- Worship in Love
- Worship in the Beauty of Holiness
- Idol Worship
- Worship as a Lifestyle
- Worship in Reverence & Devotion
- Worship to Draw Near and to Pursue God
- Worship in Prayer
- Worship in Warfare

- Worship in Healing
- Worship in Offerings
- Worship is in Your Future
- The Song of Worship

What is worship?

<u>**Worship:**</u>

To love God in the highest degree;
To regard with the utmost esteem, and
To acknowledge His worthiness

Worship in Love

And now abide faith, hope, love, these three;
but the greatest of these is love.
1 Corinthians 13:13

The nucleus of worship is love. The motivation of everything we do should be centered on love for God, and love for our fellowman. This is a simple fact: Worship is love; God is love. God's love is unconditional - Agape love.

John 3:16

For God so loved the world that He gave His only begotten Son, that whoever believes in Him should not perish but have everlasting life.

This is a familiar scripture; right? The reality is God loved us first, so why not return the same love to Him through worship?

1 John 4:10

In this is love, not that we loved God, but that He loved us and sent His Son to be the propitiation for our sins.

The following three types of worship set the groundwork for the others:

- Sebazomai Worship – Love greatly; to venerate
- Shachah Worship – Love and exalt Him as Lord; bow before Him
- Proskuneo Worship - Love as Master and prostrate before Him

SEBAZOMAI WORSHIP

Strong's Concordance #4573, Greek (Sebazomai)

Pronounced, (seb-ad'-zom-ahee)

- To venerate and adore in worship

Sebazomai worship is love expressed by reverence and adoration to God. It is through this worship that we must reverence God for who He is: Great and awesome. What does it mean to reverence and adore?

- Reverence
  - » A feeling of profound respect often mingled with awe and affection
  - » An act of respect and obeisance
- Adore
  - » To **love** and **honor** with **intense devotion**
  - » Latin: ad = **to**; orare = **speak** or **pray**

Prayer is a form of worship. To adore God in worship is to speak and pray to Him and allow Him to speak to us through His Word, and through His Spirit.

Psalm 89:7 says:
God is greatly to be feared in the assembly of the saints, and to be held in reverence by all those around Him.

The assembly of saints in this scripture is referring to the angels around His throne, and simply put, if the angels reverence God around His throne, certainly should we, His redeemed people.

It cannot be reiterated enough how important it is to keep our hearts pure and in love with God every day. Inherently, both the Old and New Testament direct us to this theory of great love.

Moses says to the Children of Israel:

Deuteronomy 30:20
20) "That you may love the LORD your God, that you may obey His voice, and that you may cling to Him, for He is your life, and the length of your days; and that you may dwell in the land which the LORD swore to your fathers, to Abraham, Isaac, and Jacob, to give them."

When asked by a lawyer, what is the foremost commandment of all, Jesus' reply was:

Mark 12:29-31

29) Jesus answered him, "The first of all the commandments is: 'Hear, O Israel, the LORD our God, the LORD is one.

30) And you shall love the LORD your God with all your heart, with all your soul, with all your mind, and with all your strength.' This is the first commandment.

31) And the second, like it, is this: 'You shall love your neighbor as yourself.' There is no other commandment greater than these."

Jesus actually quoted the Jewish Shema, (Deuteronomy 6:4,5), which not only defines the Trinity of God in terms of unity, but also the extent of how we must love God: with all our heart, soul, mind, and strength, and to love our neighbor as ourselves. The love we have for God and the love we have for our neighbor is the purest type of worship; and to be unlovable in this area would greatly affect our worship to God.

SHACHAH WORSHIP

Strong's Concordance #7812, Hebrew (Shachah)

Pronounced (shaw-khaw')

- To bow down before God as an act of love, submission and reverence
- To make oneself low
- To exalt the Lord (lift Him on high) and worship (bow yourselves down low before Him) at the place of His feet.

Worship before the Battle
Joshua 5:13-15

Joshua – Servant Worshiper

So the LORD spoke to Moses face to face, as a man speaks to his friend. And he would return to the camp, but his servant Joshua, the son of Nun, a young man, did not depart from the tabernacle.
Exodus 33:11

Joshua not only loved God, but also loved being in the presence of God. As Moses' assistant, you would find him remaining in the tabernacle. Some commentators suggest that he was guarding the tabernacle, but I choose to believe that he just wanted to be in the presence of the Lord. I call Joshua a *servant worshiper*.

Joshua 5:1-15
A familiar scripture in the Bible is the story of Joshua and the battle of Jericho. As young children, we used to sing the song, "Joshua fought the battle of Jericho, and the walls came tumbling down." However, Joshua did something unique even before the battle was fought; he worshiped God in <u>Shachah worship.</u>

In preface of this worship, Joshua was commanded by God to circumcise the men who were born in the wilderness, thus keeping the covenant of circumcision, which took away the reproach of Egypt. This meant they were no longer in bondage to Egypt. In addition, the celebration of the Passover was another act that put them in alignment to be blessed by God.

In this passage, we see that Joshua is encountered by a Man with His sword drawn. This Man being the Lord, Joshua fell on his face to the earth and worshiped. Upon recognition of speaking to the Commander of the LORD's army, (which happened to be Jesus) Joshua immediately humbled himself as a <u>servant</u> <u>worshiper</u>, and asks, "What does my Lord say to His servant?"

The concentration of Shachah worship is not allowing outside influences to distract us, but humbly bowing before the Lord in anticipation of hearing what the Spirit of the Lord has to say, and in turn doing what the Spirit of the Lord asks us to do. It is in this type of worship that our senses are spiritually in tuned with God and we are able to see what others can't see and hear what others can't hear.

God was getting ready to give Joshua specific instructions on how to fight this battle, and if he hadn't taken the position of a servant worshiper, and done what was required of him, he would not have been able to "see" this Man nor "hear" what He had to say.

The first instruction given to Joshua to win this battle was not to start out fighting, but to start out worshiping.

Joshua 5:15
"Then the Commander of the LORD's army said to Joshua, 'Take your sandal off your foot, for the place where you stand is holy.' And Joshua did so."

In Eastern culture, taking one's sandals off was a sign of humility and respect. So it is with this type of worship, we must be humble and God must be respected. We must truly recognize God's position: God. Our position: servant. And our prayer to God is, "Jesus, You are Lord, and I am your servant. What are you saying unto me, your servant?" At this place of worship, your ground becomes holy. Not because of who you are, but because of who He is and His Awesome Presence; thus your enemy is defeated even before the battle. Amen!

PROSKUNEO WORSHIP

Strong's Concordance, #4352, Greek (Proskuneo)
Pronounced, (pros-koo-neh'-o)

- To prostrate oneself, bow down, do obeisance, show reverence, do homage, worship and adore.
- To show affection, similar to a dog licking his master's hand.

Proskuneo is made up of two (2) words, pros, "toward", and kuneo, "to kiss". It is an affectionate worship of humility, obeisance, and reverence.

Our mentality in this type of worship is to see God as Master and Teacher, and to see ourselves as obedient servants, willing to do whatever pleases our Master, and to remain subservient as we are taught from Him. The Bible says that Enoch had this testimony: that he pleased God. (Hebrew 11:5). We must also have this testimony as worshipers of God. As a worshiper, Jesus, in the true sense of every way, pleased His Father. (John 8:29).

Proskuneo worship is also appropriate when we are at the point of desperation and feeling overwhelmed and exhausted; even at the point of being powerless, helpless and weak. At this point, we may not know what's going on, but because we love and trust God, we will do whatever He asks of us, knowing that He is in full control and will work out everything for our good. (Romans 8:28).

What does it mean to be Master and to prostrate?

Master:
- One who rules and governs; one who has supreme dominion and power; controlling.
- To conquer or overpower, to subdue, one who has authority to control

Prostrate:
- Lying at mercy, as a supplicant.
- To totally sink; to reduce strength

What does this really mean?
To whomever you prostrate becomes your master, giving them dominion and authority over you; reducing your strength while being within their control.

Psalm 115:8 speaks of idols, the work of men's hands....

"Those who make them are like them; so is everyone who trusts in them."

Satan Tempts Jesus to prostrate
Luke 4:7-8

This same type of worship is used by Satan in order to make Jesus prostrate before him. He was trying to make Jesus powerless and subservient to him, but of course, Jesus would not allow it!

Do not worship (proskuneo) angels
The Bible is very specific in addressing the issue of not worshiping angels and commands us to worship (prostrate, love and please) God. Revelation 22:8-9, Revelation 19:10. Angels, however, bow and prostrate before the Lord. Hebrews 1:6

Worship in the Beauty
Of Holiness

One thing I have desired of the LORD, that will I seek; that I may dwell in the house of the LORD all the days of my life, to behold the beauty of the LORD and to inquire in His temple.
Psalm 27:4

Behold His Holiness

To talk about worship is to talk about God in the beauty of His holiness. To look upon God's holiness is to behold His awesome majesty and to tremble before His Presence and Power. To behold the holiness of God is to look upon His absolute moral virtue, (which is so pure) while yet acknowledging that every sin is covered by the blood of Jesus and the power of His grace.

Be Ye Holy

To worship God to the fullest extent, one must:
- Offer your body unto God as a "living sacrifice" – Romans 12:1
- Be Holy

1 Peter 1:15-16 (NIV)

15) "But just as He who called you is holy, so be holy in all you do.
16) For it is written, 'Be ye holy because I am holy.'"
(Also noted in Leviticus 11:45)

QUESTIONS
1. How does one offer his/her body?
Answer: By a spiritual act of worship.

Memory Verse – Romans 12:1 (NIV)
Therefore, I urge you, brothers, in view of God's mercy, to offer your bodies as living sacrifices, holy and pleasing to God — this is your spiritual act of worship.

111

<u>A SPIRITUAL ACT OF WORSHIP</u> is not merely a ritual activity. A spiritual act of worship is to offer your "whole" self to God through the involvement of giving your heart, your mind, your will and your whole life to God. **Worship is not ritual, but relational.**

2. **What does "offer" mean?**
   Answer: Offer = Put yourself in the service of God.
   Offer = To be given to God alone.

3. **What can we offer to God?**
   <u>Praise Offering</u> = Fruit of our lips, the giving of thanks to God.
   <u>Worship Offering</u> = Offer your "whole" self to God in service to God.

Romans 6:13 (NIV)
Do not offer the parts of your body to sin, as instruments of wicked-ness, but rather offer yourselves to God, as those who have been brought from death to life; and offer the parts of your body to Him as instruments of righteousness.

<u>A Righteous Order</u>
Notice that the Bibles says to offer our bodies as instruments of righteousness, not instruments of wickedness. There is a clarion call for a righteous order upon this earth, and this order will start with the Body of Christ offering our bodies as instruments of righteousness through the act of worship to God.

Our own righteousness is as filthy rags, however, when we present our bodies as instruments of righteousness, it becomes worship.

What is Worship?
These are the words of Jesus:

John 4:23-24

23) "But the hour is coming, and now is, when the true worshipers will worship the Father in spirit and truth; for the Father is seeking such to worship Him.
24) God is Spirit, and those who worship Him must worship in spirit and truth."

WORSHIP IN SPIRIT

Since God is seeking TRUE WORSHIPERS who must worship in spirit and truth, we must understand what is meant by spirit and truth. First of all, we must have the Spirit of God through the born-again experience. Secondly, upon cultivating our relationship with the Father, we must learn to depend on the Holy Spirit to enable us to worship God effectively in spirit.

In your personal worship time, the Holy Spirit may want you to sing spiritual songs or hymns; He may want you to recite a Psalm, or just quietly wait in His Presence.

Ephesians 5:18-19 (NKJV)

18) "And do not be drunk with wine in which is dissipation; but be filled with the Spirit,
19) speaking to one another in psalms and hymns and spiritual songs, singing and making melody in your heart to the Lord."

1 Corinthians 14:15 (NKJV)

"What is the conclusion then? I will pray with the spirit, and I will also pray with the understanding. I will sing with the spirit and I will also sing with the understanding."

Whatever the case, our worship must be with the Spirit. Our personal worship must be Spirit-led and God-breathed. What does

God-breathed mean? When God first created man, He breathed into man "breath". . .

Genesis 2:7
*And the LORD GOD formed man of the dust of the ground, and breathed into his nostrils the **breath** of life; and man became a living being.*

The word, "breath" has two meanings: Ruach and N'shamah

1. Ruach (roo'akh), (Strong's #H7306, H7307)
   - Blast
   - Exhalation
   - Wind

2. N'shamah (nesh-aw-maw) or Neshamah (Strong's #H5397)
   - Life
   - Spirit
   - Divine inspiration
   - Intellect
   - Soul (mind, will, emotions)

Can you imagine? When man was formed from the ground, he was lifeless until God exhaled a blast of life into his nostrils and he became alive! God shared breath with Adam. God shared life with Adam. He breathed into Adam divine inspiration, and intellect—This same breath, life, and intellect is shared with us as we worship the Father in spirit.

Just as God's breath blew into Adam at creation, so does the Holy Spirit blow God's breath into our being as we worship. The Holy Spirit can assist us in worship by intertwining with our spirit. It will not be of our own intellect, but the Holy Spirit's intellect; it will not be our inspiration, but divine inspiration led by the Holy Spirit. It will be God's Spirit living inside of us as we worship.

Job 33:4
"The Spirit of God has made me, and the breath of the Almighty gives me life."

Ezekiel 37:5
"Thus says the Lord God to these bones, 'Surely I will cause breath to enter you, and you shall live.'"

Jesus breathed on His disciples when He appeared to them after the resurrection.

John 20:22
And when He had said this, He breathed on them, and said to them, "Receive the Holy Spirit."

And the Word of God commands us as we have breath, we should praise the Lord!

Psalm 150:6
"Let everything that hath breath, praise the Lord!"

Even as you are reading this book, you are breathing the breath of God, so you should praise Him! God is seeking such to worship Him in spirit by asking for the assistance of the Holy Spirit. Then and only then, will our worship be:
- Full of Breath
- Full of Vitality
- Full of Life

WORSHIP IN TRUTH

Truth is very important to God, and even though He knows everything about us, we must come to Him with our imperfections and confessions and allow Him to cleanse us from all unrighteousness. 1 John 1:9.

Again, Jesus says God is seeking for true worshipers who worship in truth. What is truth? The word truth comes from the Greek word, "<u>aletheia</u>". (al-ay-thiah). As a whole word, this word means:

Truth	Reality
Sincerity	Accuracy
Integrity	Dependability
Truthfulness	Propriety
*Veracity	

*<u>Veracity</u> is the habitual observance of truth, which is an important element of worship. The habitual observance of truth comes from the standard of God's Word. When God reveals truth to you, He expects you to change, or conform to His Word. Sometimes the acknowledgment of truth cuts like a sharp knife, especially when we display behaviors that are not in alignment with God's Word; however, your acceptance to change will help you to become a better person.

Hebrews 4:12
For the word of God is quick, and powerful, and sharper than any twoedged sword, piercing even to the dividing asunder of soul and spirit, and of the joints and marrow, and is a discerner of the thoughts and intents of the heart.

Let's again analyze the word, "aletheia". When the article "a" is in front of this word, the meaning becomes negative.

Truth
a-letheia (Greek word) – Strong's' #225
lethal (English word)

*Note: Lethal is to cause death, destruction. When you put the article, "a" in front of the word lethal, it means, "**not**" to cause death or be destructive.

Truth
a - lethal
not - causing death
not - being destructive.

Thus when Jesus says we must worship in truth (aletheia), He means don't allow your worship to cause death or be destructive. How can we do this? If our hearts are not right with God our worship can become destructive.

Again, the word of God teaches us to be truthful and honor God with our hearts, not just with our lips.

Matthew 15:8-9
8) *"These people draw near to Me with their mouth, and honor Me with their lips, but their heart is far from Me.*
9) *And in vain they worship Me, teaching as doctrines the commandments of men."*

This scripture was mentioned earlier in "A Heart Condition: Praises from the Heart"; however, I want to further analyze the study of this scripture in Hebrew context. This is my paraphrase:

"These people draw near to me with their mouth and value Me with their lips, but their thoughts, feelings, and mind is far from Me. And by manipulation, unsuccessful search, and with no purpose they worship Me, teaching as doctrines the commandments of men."

Jesus called the Scribes and Pharisees, "hypocrites" because they pretend to worship God through their long prayers and fasted with awkward faces.

In other words, their hearts were not toward God, but they honored the teaching of doctrine more than the worship of God. Let us learn a lesson and draw near to honor God with true worship; not with false pretense or hypocrisy, but with a contrite and humble heart.

Worship in Truth
a – lanthano (Greek word)
latent (English word)
not – to lie hidden
not – to be dormant or inactive
not – to escape notice

When something is latent, it can be inactive for quite some time, but when it hits the surface, it can become deadly. For instance, if we are passive about not keeping a healthy immune system, we can allow sickness to stay in our bodies at a slow, inactive rate, and it escapes our notice until it is in a full deadly stage. A volcano can stay dormant for many years until one day it erupts; a bomb also can be unnoticed until it detonates.

Inasmuch, God is seeking true worshipers whose worship is not hidden, dormant or inactive, but alive and explosive. God is seeking true worshipers whose worship is proactive and truthful.

Not to escape notice really means the opposite; you want to engage in worship so God notices you. Your worship becomes attractive (comely) to God. Psalms 147:1 says your praise is beautiful; your worship can be beautiful, too.

King David says in Psalm 51:6
"Behold, You desire truth in the inward parts, and in the hidden part You will make me to know wisdom."

Worship in Truth
a – lanthano (Greek word)
lethargy (English word)
not – to be in a deep sleep, or slumber
not – to be in a trance, or stupor

This means our worship should not be inattentive, but it must be devoted to quality time spent with God. We must not be in a trance, but accurate and watchful.

The five foolish virgins were not attentive or watchful as they did not have their lamps trimmed with enough oil, thus their lamps were going out and they were not able to meet the Bridegroom when He came. Matthew 25:1-13

Prayer is another form of worship. Jesus said to His disciples after finding them sleeping, "What? Could you not watch with Me one hour?" Matthew 26:40

WHO ARE THE TRUE WORSHIPERS?
The Bible says that God is seeking for true worshipers. The word, "**seeking**", in the Greek is "**zeteo**" (dzay-teh'-o), (#G2212), which means "**to search for something hidden**". God is searching for true worshipers like He's searching for hidden treasure. Could He be searching for you? **When you accept Jesus Christ as your Personal Savior, you become a worshiper, and you become valuable to God!**

What is the definition of a True Worshiper?

True:
- Faithful, real, honest, sincere, integrity
- To conform to the reality of God's word
- To be truthful

Worshiper:

The word, "worshiper" is the Greek word, "**Proskunetes**", which means to be an "**Adorer**". Remember what we learned about the word, "adore"?

- **Adore**
  » To **love** and **honor** with **intense devotion**
  » Latin: ad = **to**; orare = **speak** or **pray**.

As we put all these things together, we come up with this definition:

TRUE WORSHIPER:

One who loves and honors God with intense devotion. One who speaks or prays to God in honesty, sincerity and integrity, while conforming to the reality of God's word and executing His will.

CONCLUSION

In summary, when Jesus said, "......true worshipers will worship the Father in spirit and truth", He means that the true worshiper's worship is genuine and sincere; alive with divine inspiration; does not cause death or destruction, and does not go unnoticed.

Truly the Father is seeking such to worship Him.

Christ-Centered Worship
Philippians 3:3

For we are the circumcision; who worship God in the Spirit; rejoice in Christ Jesus, and have no confidence in the flesh.

The circumcision mentioned here is not the cutting of the flesh, but the cutting of the heart, putting away all carnality, and having no confidence in the flesh, but rather worshiping in the Spirit. The main focus of our worship must be Christ-centered. It must not be based on our own achievements and anointing but based solely on the works of Christ by exalting Him, and honoring God.

Paul could have put confidence in all of his achievements, but he counted them rubbish that he may gain Christ. **Philippians 3:8**

Romans 2:28-29

28) "For he is not a Jew who is one outwardly, nor is circumcision that which is outward in the flesh;
29) but he is a Jew who is one inwardly; and circumcision is that of the heart, in the Spirit, not in the letter; whose praise is not from men but from God."

Honest Worship

When we, in honesty, yield our true selves to God in worship, His love will be so overwhelming that we forget about ourselves and concentrate on Him; and as a reward we will receive a revelation of His desires, His heart, and His plans for our lives.

Worship is Important To God

There are many scriptures that point to the fact that worship is important to God.

- WORSHIP is so important to God that the first two commandments deal with worshiping the One and only True God, instead of idols.

Exodus 20:3
3) "You shall have no other gods before Me."
4) "You shall not make for yourself a carved image."
5) "You shall not bow down to them nor serve them."

- WORSHIP is so important to God that the Lord's Prayer starts with worship and ends in worship.

Matthew 6:9,10,13
9) Our Father in heaven, Hallowed be Your name.
10) Your kingdom come. Your will be done on earth as it is in heaven.
13) For Yours is the kingdom and the power and the glory forever. Amen.

- WORSHIP is so important to Jesus that He said this about Mary (who was sitting at His feet): One thing is needful: that good part (worship).

Luke 10:42
But one thing is needed, and Mary has chosen that good part, which will not be taken away from her.

- WORSHIP is so important that Lucifer challenged Jesus to worship him instead of the worship of God.

Matthew 4:5-11

10) Then Jesus said to him, "Away with you, Satan! For it is written, 'You shall worship the LORD your God, and Him only you shall serve.'"

Let us follow Jesus' example by resisting the devil and staying true to God alone in our service of worship.

IDOL WORSHIP

You shall have no other gods before Me.
Exodus 20:3

As we continue to study about worship, we must keep in mind on a consistent basis that the essence of our worship is to be directed toward the Father, and honoring the works of Christ. In addition, worship must include offering our bodies as living sacrifices, holy and pleasing in service to God. This is our spiritual act of worship. However, in order for our worship to be in the purest sense there must first be a removal of all forms of idol worship. There can be no true worship unless there is the removal of false worship.

FIRST THINGS FIRST – DESTROY FALSE WORSHIP

When the Children of Israel were about to enter the Promise Land, God knew that it was easy persuasion for them to be influenced by false gods. However, in order to encounter true worship, they had to annihilate all types of false worship.

In Deuteronomy 12 God gives specific instructions to His people: Utterly destroy all places of false worship!! The command was not just to destroy, but to "<u>utterly</u>" destroy!!!

Read Deuteronomy 12:1-5

Deuteronomy 12:4
"You shall not worship the LORD your God with such things."

The people who inhabited the Promise Land, the Canaanites, practiced false worship. They did this by worshiping at these places:
- The High Mountains
- The Hills
- Under every green tree

124

Why was this so? The mountains or hills were thought to be the home of a god, and by ascending the mountain, the worship was symbolic of being closer to a deity. In addition, worshiping under every green tree was thought to be sacred and symbolized fertility.

Elements of Canaan worship were these:
- Altars
- Pillars
- Wooden Images
- Carved Images

Canaan worship also included the act of human sacrifices. God commanded that these things be not so with His people. They were not even permitted to "inquire" anything about idol worship because it would become too enticing and a snare to them.

Deuteronomy 12:30-32

PLACES OF GODLY WORSHIP
God established places for the Children of Israel to worship:
- Mount Ebal – Deuteronomy 27:1-8, Joshua 8:30-35
- Shechem – Joshua 24:1-28
- Shiloh – Joshua 18:1

An altar was to be built by whole stones, whitewashed with lime, and written very plainly on the stones were all the words of the Law.

God did not want the Children of Israel to mix heathen worship with Godly worship. It is recorded in later books, that because the Israelites didn't get rid of the Canaanites, the Hittites, and all those "ites" that they in fact did mix heathen worship with the worship of God.

IDOL WORSHIP – Eidolon, Greek/Strong's #1497 (I-do-lon)

Eidolon is the worship of a heathen god. Did you know that when a King came into office, one of the best things he did for his kingdom was totally annihilate idol worship?

2 Kings 22:1-11

King Josiah became King at the tender age of 8 years old, and he did what was right in the sight of the Lord by walking in the ways of his father, David; however great wrath and calamity were on the people because they were involved in false worship.

2 Kings 23:1-25

When Josiah became aware of these idolatrous acts, he got rid of every image and altar he could find. The following things were torn down:

- Idols in the temple (verses 4-6)
- Idolatrous priests (verses 5,8)
- The practice of sodomy and prostitution in the temple (verse 7)
- The practice of astrology (verse 5)
- The ritual sacrifices of children (verse 10)
- He broke down altars of all idols:
  - » Baal
  - » Asherah
  - » Topheth
  - » Molech
  - » Ashtoreth & Milcom
  - » Chemosh
- He killed people who consulted spiritists and mediums
- Josiah brought back all the Levitical priests
- Josiah restored the Passover

These are the words of Jesus: "You cannot serve God and mammon". The type of god mentioned in this passage is the god of money, but it can apply to any particular god. Read Matthew 6:24

Let's take a moment and think about this: What types of idols are in our lives that we need to get rid of? An idol doesn't necessarily have to be an image; it could be a person, a job, money, a compulsive behavior or attitude.

Once these idols are identified, what must we do about them? Answer: Totally annihilate them in the name of the Jesus! The Bible says in Matthew 18:8-9 that if our hand or foot causes us to sin, cut it off. We must get rid of anything and everything that takes the place of the worship of God.

VARIOUS FORMS OF FALSE WORSHIP
There are many forms of worship; however, before we explore what the "true" forms of worship are, we are going to identify what the "false" forms of worship are so that we can avoid them.

1. Will Worship – Ethelothreskeia, Greek/Strong's #1479
Pronounced (eth-el-oth-race-ki'-ah)
- This type of worship is unwarranted, unnecessary and unreasonable. It is based on an individual's voluntary will to display religious rules and regulations as worship, instead of worship to God.
- This type of worship is sanctimonious, which is a false profession of lip service and two-facedness; showing an outwardly display of devoutness of rituals instead of an inward devotion to God. This type of worship is rooted in pride, false humility, and hypocrisy.
- This type of worship is self-imposed worship by showing neglect to the body, which has no value. This type of worship only brings attention to oneself instead of God.

The Colossians Church – Will Worship

The worship in the Colossians church was based on following rules and human teachings. These rules required strong devotion and humiliation to the body and often displayed a false sense of humility and pride.

Keep in mind that our worship must be Christ-centered; therefore Paul urges the Colossians church that as they have received Christ, to walk in Him or follow Him by being rooted, built up, and established in the faith, not by the observances of the new moon, festivals, or a holy day or the worship of angels.

Read Colossian 2:6-10

Paul's message to this church was that Jesus had taken away their sins, having nailed them to the cross; so in essence, they didn't have to flaunt their worship by keeping rules and regulations.

Paul's argument was this:

Colossians 2:20
Therefore if you died with Christ from the basic principles of the world, why as though living in the world, do you subject yourselves to regulations—

Colossians 2:23 (NIV)
Such regulations indeed have an appearance of wisdom, with their self-imposed worship, their false humility, and their harsh treatment of the body, but they lack any value in restraining sensual indulgence.

These prideful acts certainly looked good, but they had no value in restraining the flesh.

Proverbs 16:18 says
Pride goes before destruction and a haughty spirit before a fall.

Lucifer, the Master of Will Worship

Lucifer was a will-worshiper bringing attention to himself. God created him to carry the music and appointed him to conduct worship in Heaven. The following is some information to help us learn the lesson of humility.

- Lucifer's Description (Ezekiel 28:12-13)
  - » Seal of perfection
  - » Full of wisdom
  - » Perfect in beauty
    - A priest fully clothed with precious stones and instruments of music could be heard from him such as timbrels, pipes, harps, flutes, and trumpets.
- Lucifer's Role (Ezekiel 28:14)
  - » The Anointed Cherub who covers –
    - Lucifer's name means "Light Bearer" or "Shining One"
    - He held a high office with authority and responsibility to protect and defend the Holy Mountain of God.
    - Sheriff or policeman is the English form of Cherub.
  - » Minister of Music in Heaven –
    - His role was leading Heaven's choir in the worship among the Throne of the Most High.
- Satan's Fall – Isaiah 14:12-17 & Ezekiel 28:16-19
  - » Lucifer's name changed to Satan (devil) and he was cast out of Heaven because of pride, admiring his own beauty and wanting to be on the Throne instead of worshiping at the Throne.
  - » In Isaiah, The "5" I-Will's, are the downfall of Lucifer:
    - I will ascend into the Heaven.
    - I will exalt my throne above the stars of God.
    - I will also sit on the mount of the congregation on the farthest sides of the North.
    - I will ascend above the heights of the clouds.
    - I will be like the Most High.
  - » Rather than worshiping God from his inner most being, Lucifer was looking on the outside. Lucifer was looking at his

beauty and position—he was not worshiping God. Lucifer was looking at his anointing—he was not worshiping God.

» Because of his pride, he was cast out of Heaven.

- Ezekiel 28:17 – Your heart was lifted up because of your beauty; you corrupted your wisdom for the sake of your splendor.

» Satan no longer was perfected in wisdom and beauty but because of pride, he became a horror and the sound of song was taken away from him.

- Ezekiel 28:19 – *All who knew you among the peoples are astonished at you; you have become a horror.*
- Ezekiel 26:13 – *I will put an end to the sound of your songs, and the sound of your harps shall be heard no more.* (Also noted in Revelations 18:22-23)

Lessons Learned

- Humility – Let us not be prideful, but stay humble before God.
- A Word to Choir Members:
  » As we have been given the responsibility to lead the congregation in praise and worship, let us not glory in the position which God has given us, but stay faithful to the call of worship.

2. Image Worship – Eidololatreia, Greek/Strong's #1495
Pronounced (I-do-lol-at-ri'-ah)

Eidololatreia worship is a pre-existing image or idol set up for worship. This type of worship goes against the commandments of God, and as we engage in this type of worship, we become estranged or separated from God and allow ourselves to be under the control of what is worshiped.

The Bible teaches us that we should not trust in or worship idols that are set up in our lives, but trust in our God in Heaven. In fact, the

Bible says those who make idols are just like them, having eyes, but can't see, and ears, but can't hear.

Read Psalm 115:3-11
This an excellent passage, for it teaches us not to trust in material things, (silver or gold) or images; however, it mentions three (3) times that we should trust in the LORD, for He is our help and shield.

The Three Hebrew Boys were tested in eidololatreia worship when Nebuchadnezzar the King set up an image of gold that was to be worshiped. And as we know the story, their worship remained true to the One and Only God of Heaven! Nebuchadnezzar agreed:

Daniel 3:28
"Nebuchadnezzar spoke, saying, 'Blessed be the God of Shadrach, Meshach, and Abed-Nego, who sent His Angel and delivered His servants who trusted in Him, and they have frustrated the king's word, and yielded their bodies, that they should not serve nor worship any god except their own God'!"

3. Atsab Worship – Hebrew/Strong's #6087
Pronounced (Aw-tsab')

This type of worship is to carve or fashion an idol. This is a self-existing idol, which we impose on ourselves, choosing rather to believe the lie of our minds, rather than trust God. Inasmuch, this creates strongholds, illusions and deception. These things must be broken by the weapons of warfare through the Word of God and the Blood of Jesus as stated in 2 Corinthians 10:3-6.

Worship as a Lifestyle
(The Character of Worship)

As Mary broke the alabaster box and the aroma fragrantly filled the room where Jesus was sitting, so must the aroma of our worship fill the places where we sit, whether this is a classroom, the work environment, or the home; our character must exude worship. Yes, worship has a character, and this character stems from the act of giving homage to God.

The Character of Worship
Allegiance devotion   loyalty   fidelity   reverence   faithfulness

Constancy dedication respect service obeisance consecration

L O V E

Another important fact to remember is that when we serve God, we worship God. Psalm 100 expresses this so beautifully, and it shows us the type of attitude we should have as we worship:

Psalm 100:1-2 (NKJV)
1) *Make a joyful shout to the LORD, all you lands!*
2) ***Serve*** *the LORD with gladness; come before His presence with singing.*

Psalm 100:1-2 (NIV)
1) *Shout for joy to the LORD, all the earth,*
2) ***Worship*** *the LORD with gladness; come before Him with joyful songs.*

The word, serve is the Hebrew word, "<u>Abad</u>" (ah-vahd), Strong's Concordance, #5647, which means to be a servant or to worship.

When we <u>serve God</u> in the capacity for which He calls us, we are <u>worshiping God</u>. Amen!

The fruit of the Spirit is one fruit, but has many components; worship has many elements that makeup worship—a lifestyle of worship.

Ponder this interesting fact – God told Moses to give Pharaoh this message: "Let My people go so they can <u>*worship*</u> Me in the wilderness."

Exodus 5:1
Afterward Moses and Aaron went in and told Pharaoh, "Thus says the LORD God of Israel: 'Let My people go, that they may <u>hold a feast</u> to Me in the wilderness.'"

Note: A feast is a community activity where the people would stop their normal activities to offer thanksgiving. It is a joyous time of eating and <u>*worship*</u>.

God is saying this:
- "My people are in bondage, and I want them to come and hold a feast and worship Me."
- "I want to get my people out of bondage to worship Me."
- "I want My people out of bondage to worship."

(I hope you are getting the picture)

God is saying to you today:
- God wants to joyously fellowship with you through a relationship of worship and deliver you from years of bondage so you can enjoy life!

Worship in Reverence and Devotion

Therefore, since we are receiving a kingdom which cannot be shaken, let us have grace, by which we may serve God acceptably with reverence and godly fear.

Hebrews 12:28

It is a wonderful thing to reverence and be in awe of God; to acknowledge Him in amazement of His greatness, and to confess that He is your Lord. To worship God in this way is called, "Yadah Worship". It means to extend your hands in reverence to God; to know Him intimately; to understand His ways, and to desire Him and Him alone. It means that you desire no one greater. Moses wanted to know God in this way when he said, "Please, show me Your glory." Exodus 33:18

Yadah Worship
(Yaw-daw), Hebrew #3034

The word "yad" means an opened hand. We learned in our "praise" study that to give God a "Yadah Praise" was to extend the hands in thanksgiving to God for what He has done; however, to "Yadah" in worship is to extend the hands in worship as **an act of reverence and yielding oneself to God, and to know Him intimately**.

Note:
- To lift your hands in worship is to lay down your weapons; similar to when a police officer has caught a thief and commands him to lay down his weapon, so must we lay down our weapons before God. Whether it is pride, selfishness, or rebellion, or arrogance; lay them down as an act of surrender to God.
- To worship God with extended hands is to submit your life to Him.
- Lifting your hands in prayer is similar to extending your hands in worship.

Scriptures: Psalm 134: 2; Psalm 141:2; and Psalm 143:6

Eusebeo Worship
(Yoo-seb-eh'-o), Greek #2151
- To worship God in respectfulness.
- To worship God through devotion.
- To worship God in commitment and faithfulness.

In view of having a deeper relationship with God through worship, one of the first lessons learned is to give God the respect He deserves. Most importantly, when God gives you an assignment, He must be shown respect. Why? Because He is God and you are not and as He is respected, you will honor Him in obedience. For example, when Moses' attention was captured through the burning bush experience, the first thing God required of Moses was respect.

Exodus 3:5
"Then He said, 'Do not draw near this place. Take your sandals off your feet, for the place where you stand is holy ground'".

In Eastern culture, taking off one's shoes was a sign of respect. God commanded Moses to take off his sandals. After a display of respect was shown, God revealed Himself to Moses and began to share His heart as to the deliverance of the Children of Israel. And so it is with us, once God sees our respect, he can share deeper revelation and purpose for our lives.

When Joseph was tempted by Potiphar's wife to commit sin, his lifestyle of worship remained devout and faithful to God. We can see that God used Joseph in a mighty way. Genesis 39:7-12

When a decree went out that no one petition any god except Darius, Daniel went straight to his room; knelt, prayed and gave thanks to

God as usual. He did not allow the circumstances to dictate his worship; he stayed focused and committed. Daniel 6:7-8

Note:

- Most people view devotion or commitment to God as of no importance; God looks upon this character as significant.
- How is your lifestyle of worship? Are you committed to living holy and being faithful to God in your daily living, come what may? Selah. Pause and think of that.

Other Scriptures: Hebrews 3:2; Numbers 32:12; Deuteronomy 1:36

Worship to Draw Near and to Pursue God

It is good for me to draw near to God; I have put my trust in the
LORD GOD, that I may declare all Your works.
Psalm 73:28

Abraham knew that God was going to destroy Sodom and Gomorrah, but he <u>came near to God</u> for a purpose, which was to make a request that the righteous (his nephew, Lot) might not be destroyed with the wicked.

Genesis 18:23
"And Abraham came near and said, 'Would You destroy the righteous with the wicked'?"

When Abraham knew that he had God's attention, he began to speak kindly in intercession for the sake of his nephew. What Abraham was doing was speaking <u>an argument by reversal</u>. It wasn't that God changed his mind about the judgment of Sodom and Gomorrah; it was the fact that the judgment of Lot was reversed because Abraham made intercession for him.

<u>**Nagash Worship**</u>
(Naw-gash'), Hebrew #5066
- To cause to draw near for a purpose.
- To speak kindly for a cause.
- To produce an argument by reversal.

We can do the same for our families and friends in worship to the Father. We can draw near to God in faith, believing that He is a God that answers prayers. This is by no means trying to coerce God in doing things our way, but rather drawing close to God to know His will.

Hebrews 10:22

Let us draw near with a true heart in full assurance of faith, having our hearts sprinkled from an evil conscience and our bodies washed with pure water.

Drawing near to God is being confident that our faith will place us in position to hear God and to intercede for others.

Darash Worship

(daw-rash'), Hebrew #1875

- To pursue God.
- To seek after and search for the counsel of God.
- To make inquisition.

Darash worship; a worship of sacrifice; a worship displayed in earnest desperation for God to reveal truth and direction; a worship to receive counsel from God. This is the type of worship where the preparation of your heart is set on the pursuit of God and searching for Him with all your heart. It is to search for God diligently, painstakingly, and "early" in the morning. This also could mean "early" in your situation.

Jeremiah 29:13

And you will seek Me and find Me, when you search for Me with all your heart.

Psalm 63:1-2

1) O GOD, You are my God; early will I seek You; my soul thirsts for You; my flesh longs for You in a dry and thirsty land where there is no water.
2) So I have looked for You in the sanctuary to see Your power and Your glory.

Note

The word, "seek" in Psalm 63 is Shachar, Hebrew #7836, which means to seek after God; to dawn, early at any task, to seek early with the implication of earnestness; to seek by the extension; to search for painstakingly.

Great examples:
King Hezekiah – 2 Chronicles 31:20-21
- God will not forsake those who seek Him in this type of worship. Psalm 9:10
- Those who seek the Lord can rejoice in Him! Psalm 40:16
- David sets his heart to seek God. Psalm 27:4, 7-9
- To worship God in this way delivers you from fear! Psalm 34:4
- To worship God in this way delivers you from lack! Psalm 34:10

The Bible says that we become evil when we don't prepare our hearts to seek the LORD. II Chronicles 12:14

To Make Inquisitions
Some people feel uncomfortable about asking questions to God; however, God views this differently. It is repeated all through scripture about understanding and knowing what the will of the Lord is, and how can we know unless we take time in worship to inquire of the Lord? God may not tell us everything, but He will reveal what is necessary.

Darash worship helps you to receive God's counsel. It may take some effort in waiting upon Him, but your efforts are truly rewarded.

Proverbs 19:20-21
The Lord's Counsel Will Stand

Proverbs 1:24-26
Calamity is the results of not seeking the counsel of God.

Proverbs 20:18
Plans are established by counsel; by wise counsel wage war.

David Inquires of the Lord
2 Samuel 5:17-25

On two separate occasions, the Philistines were after David in the Valley of Rephaim. On both occasions, the Bible specifically says, "David inquired of the LORD". God's answer the first time was, "Go up, for I will doubtless deliver the Philistines into your hand." God counseled David a little differently the second time; the LORD says, "You shall not go up, circle behind them, and come upon them in front of the mulberry trees." Darash worship gave David the upper hand every time.

Would you like a provision of knowledge on what to do in certain situations? Are you confused and don't know what to do? Take time to worship. God is always available to provide an answer. God is not predictable; He may direct you to do something one way, and at another time, direct you differently. Whatever the case, the emphasis is inquiring of the LORD and doing exactly what He says. Amen!

Worship in Prayer

If My people who are called by My name will humble themselves and pray and seek My face, and turn from their wicked ways, then I will hear from heaven, and will forgive their sin and heal their land.
2 Chronicles 7:14-16

Proseuche Worship
(pros-yoo-khay') Greek, #4335
- To worship in prayer by earnest oratory (speaking) to God
- To worship in prayer by public expression
- To publicly pray in a chapel; public prayer

"A man's word is his bond" was a phrase used frequently back in the day. This meant, of course, that a person of this character did what he said, and said what he did. His words could be trusted and was very dependable.

God's word can be trusted, especially when it is spoken by Him. The Bible says our God is a God of His word—what He says He does.

Numbers 23:19
God is not a man, that He should lie; nor a son of man, that He should repent. Has He said, and will He not do? Or has He spoken, and will He not make it good?

There is something very unique about speaking and praying God's word. Jesus, Himself says this about His words:

John 6:63
"It is the Spirit who gives life; the flesh profits nothing. The words that I speak to you are spirit, and they are life."

Why is speaking God's word in prayer so special?
- The angels heed the voice of His word. Read **Psalm 103:20**.
- His word runs very swiftly – **Psalm 147:15**
- God's word is life and health – **Proverbs 4:20-22**
- God says to speak His word, "faithfully" – **Jeremiah 23:28**
- God's word is alive and powerful – **Hebrews 4:12**

We must also understand that as we speak the word of God, it must be mixed with faith or it doesn't profit. Hebrews 4:2

God magnifies His Word even above all His name..............

I will worship toward Your holy temple, and praise Your name
For Your lovingkindness and Your truth;
For You have magnified Your word above all Your name.
Psalm 138:2

Question: Why is worshiping this way so special?
Answer: The Word of God prayed publicly puts a demand on God's Presence.

Proseuche Worship Brings Freedom
Acts 12:1-19

Peter was kept in prison because Herod the king saw that it pleased the Jews. However, constant prayer was offered on his behalf.

Acts 12:5
"Peter was therefore kept in prison, but constant prayer was offered to God for him by the church."

Because of this prayer and worship, some unusually supernatural things happened for Peter:
- An angel of the Lord visited Peter in prison

- Peter's chains fell off his hands
- Peter thought he was dreaming, but the angel told him to put on his clothes and shoes and follow him. Peter followed him until they came to an iron gate.
- The gate miraculously opened to them on its own accord.

Miracles happen when believers come together in worship and prayer!

Proserchomai Worship
(pros-er'-khom-ahee) – Greek, #4334
- To approach
- To come near, draw near to worship
- To assent/consent (be in agreement)

Have you ever sensed a need to come up higher in the Lord? Have you ever felt a need to get alone and pray? Do not ignore this beckoning because it is God's Spirit calling you to a higher level in worship through prayer.

In this type of worship, we should purposefully take time to withdraw from distractions and give God our full attention. When we do this, the Lord will reveal any guidance or correction necessary to come up to a higher level. This type of worship requires being in 100% agreement with God, which means we must agree with His word, commandments, and the guidance of the Holy Spirit.

Moses and Others are Called to Approach God
Exodus 24:1-18

It is important, as we feel the prompting of the Holy Spirit beckoning us to come before God's presence, that we spend quality time in worship. We may not know all the reasons for this prompting, but as stated before, it will definitely be revealed to us.

In Exodus 24, Moses and others were specifically told to come up to the mountain and worship from afar.

Exodus 24:1-2
1) "Now He said to Moses, 'Come up to the LORD, you and Aaron, Nadab and Abihu, and seventy of the elders of Israel, and worship from afar.
2) And Moses alone shall come near the LORD, but they shall not come near, nor shall the people go up with him.'"

- ▪ **Note**:
  The word, worship in verse 1, is actually the Hebrew word, <u>Shachah</u>, which means to make oneself low; to bow down as an act of submission; however, this is an excellent illustration of <u>Proserchomai</u> worship, which means to approach and draw near.

<u>**Worship, "from afar"**</u>
Aaron, Nadab, Abihu, and the 70 elders were to worship from afar, meaning they were <u>*separated apart*</u> from the Children of Israel to a specific point in the mountain, and for a specific reason. These chief leaders were allowed to see the God of Israel (as they saw the feet of God), and this worship experience allowed them to enjoy a covenant meal with God. This covenant meal also solidified their leadership, in relationship to the Children of Israel (verses 9-11).

However, Moses was called to come up higher on the mountain to worship – he was to draw near to God for a specific reason, and for a longer period of time. It is interesting to note that God gradually calls Moses up on the mountain. At one point of the mountain, he is given the tablets of stone, and then as a cloud covers him, he waits for God another 6 days. On the 7th day, God calls him again, and he comes out of the midst of the cloud, and goes up further to the mountain and stays there for 40 days and 40 nights (verses 12-18).

Why was God treating Moses in such a way? The reason is that God was getting ready to reveal to Moses a heavenly vision that laid out the plan for the Tabernacle. God needed Moses' full attention as well as his disposition to be prepared to receive such revelation. Moses' ascent up the mountain was his way of becoming in agreement with what God needed to do upon the earth (which was to build the Tabernacle).

Inasmuch, when you are in "Proserchomai worship", there will be those that will worship with you at one point, but when God calls you to a higher level, friends, family, brothers and sisters must remain, and you must go up. It is at this point that you are in the secret place of the Most High and He will reveal to you what is necessary to take you to the next level of your walk with Him.

Yes, this is alone-time with God. It may cause you to wait on Him in prayer; maybe 1, 2, 3 days; maybe 40 days. But know this; your waiting will not be in vain. Whatever God calls you to do, do it! Your spiritual sensitivity will increase to higher heights and your spiritual journey will take you to a deeper experience with God that you will never ever forget.

Baqash Worship
Pronounced, (baw-kash) – Hebrew, #1245
- To search out specifically through prayer or worship
- To strive after God
- To ask, beg, beseech, enquire, require

Have you ever heard of cause and effect? Have you ever stopped to think why something is happening in your life and you can't seem to put your finger on it? This is the time for Baqash worship. It is a worship of inquiry – to ask a question or to seek for truth.

2 SAMUEL 21:1

King David couldn't figure out why there was famine in the land for three (3) years. And the Bible says "David inquired of the LORD." In essence, he asked God the reason why this was happening. The Lord's answer: "It is because of Saul and his bloodthirsty house, because he killed the Gibeonites."

God doesn't owe us any answers. It is totally up to His sovereign will whether He answers us or not. Since there was famine in the land, David knew there was a cause, and he was right. Many, many years ago, the Gibeonites were sworn protection by Joshua, and this promise could not be broken; however, King Saul sought to kill the Gibeonites. His actions caused this famine to be in the land.

David's inquiry through prayer and worship pointed him in the right direction to make restitution, and after that, God heeded the prayer for the land (2 Samuel 21:14).

Do you have any inquiries that you want settled in your life? Pray about it, and worship God, He will work things out for your good.

Proseuchomai Worship
Pronounced, (Pros-yoo'-khom-ahee) – Greek, #4336
- Pros = To come forward in the direction of God (Greek #4314)
- Euchomai = To ask for God's will. (Greek #2172)
- To endure in prayer and supplication
- To press in, to make a demand, to make an appeal

Please note: Pro<u>seu</u>chomai is not to be confused with "Pro<u>ser</u>chomai"

Similar to Darash worship, this worship demands spending solitaire, alone-time with God, early before the dawning. A serious worshiper who needs to press in and make an appeal before God would benefit from this experience.

This type of worship was stable for Jesus, and there are numerous, countless scriptures that describe this well-known habit. Jesus is **The True Example of a Worshiper.**

PRAYER IS A FORM OF WORSHIP

Prayer is a form of worship. It is easy to think that our will makes a difference in this worship; but Jesus portrays the opposite. In fact, He prayed three (3) times to the Father, saying not My will, but Thy will be done. Matthew 26:36-39, 42, 44, and Mark 1:35. So if you're going to worship in "proseuchomai worship", your bend should be toward the will of God.

There are many other things to consider in this worship. This type of worship:

- Demands faith to believe and receive the promises of God. Mark 11:24
- Requires the act of forgiveness toward any. Mark 11:25
- Requires watchfulness and discernment. Mark 13:33, Mark 14:38
- Blesses and prays for those who despitefully use you. Luke 6:28
- Reflects an exuberant countenance being alone with God. Luke 9:29
- Requires that you pray without ceasing and never give up! Luke 18:1, and 1 Thessalonians 5:17

Jesus stayed in prayer and worship all night before He chose his disciples.

Luke 6:12

"Now it came to pass in those days that He went out to the mountain to pray, and continued all night in prayer to God."

DAVID WORSHIPS IN PRAYER FOR GOD'S WILL

David prayed and fasted in making an appeal for God's will concerning the life of his son, born to him from Bathsheba. In the acceptance of God's sovereignty, David says,

2 Samuel 12:22-23

22) *And he said*, "While the child was alive, I fasted and wept; for I said, 'Who can tell whether the LORD will be gracious to me, that the child may live?'
23) But now he is dead; why should I fast? Can I bring him back again? I shall go to him, but he shall not return to me'."

When David found out that the child was dead, the Bible said he went into the house of the LORD and worshiped (2 Samuel 12:20).

So, remember; being in prayer is being in worship. It is not necessarily getting our prayers answered as we would; but communicating with The Sovereign God whose will must be done on Earth as it is in Heaven is most important.

Athar Worship

Pronounced, (aw-thar') – Hebrew, #6279
- To burn incense in worship
- To intercede in prayer
- To entreat in prayer
- To reciprocally listen to prayer

According to the Tabernacle of Moses, to burn incense meant you were a priest ministering in the Holy Place; that an animal was killed and blood was shed, and a sacrifice was made. This meant that you were ceremonially cleansed, and you partook of the Bread of His Presence and enjoyed the light from the golden candlestick. I said all that to say this: when you finally came to burn incense, it meant that you were in the position to pray and intercede on behalf of others.

It took a while for me to catch on as I studied about Athar Worship, but in summary, this it what it means to worship in this way:

- Because you have presented yourself holy unto God, He delights in you.
- Because He delights in your worship, He "graciously" grants your prayer of intercession and entreaty, and the person you are praying for receives the benefit of God's favor.

In other words, God will delight in your worship of Him, and He will listen to your prayer of intercession and bless the other person. Now remember this, YOU "CANNOT" WORSHIP FOR SOMEONE ELSE, BUT YOU "CAN" INTERCEDE FOR SOMEONE ELSE. In this type of worship, God looks favorably on someone else because of your entreat and intercession. You, of course, do not have any power to do anything; however, God's grace and mercy and sovereignty is working big time upon the one you're interceding for. God is the one who is "Reciprocally listening to prayer".

Genesis 25:21
"Now Isaac pleaded with the LORD for his wife, because she was barren; and the LORD granted his plea, and Rebekah his wife conceived."

MANASSEH INQUIRED GOD FOR HIMSELF
2 Chronicles 33:12-14

King Manasseh did evil in the sight of the Lord (even though his father, King Hezekiah was a good king). God spoke to Manasseh about his behavior, but he wouldn't listen. As a result, the Army of the King of Assyria came and bound him with fetters.

Through all his affliction, the Bible says Manasseh implored and became greatly humbled and God gave him his kingdom back.........
then Manasseh knew that the LORD was God.

Have you ever felt like you dropped the ball; missed the anointing because of your pride, arrogance, and disobedience. I think we've all been there sometime in our life. In Athar worship, you can inquire of the Lord and entreat God for yourself. This type of worship will definitely give you a heart of humility and place you in the right attitude toward God.

Worship in Warfare

For the weapons of our warfare are not carnal but
mighty in God for pulling down strongholds.
2 Corinthians 10:4

Worship can be so rejuvenating and refreshing. At times, you may think you've gone beyond the clouds and kissed your Creator and become so satiated with His love that you never want to leave this place of bliss and nirvana. However, did you know that the same God that shows you His wonder is the same God of warfare?

Tsaba / Tsebaah Worship
Pronounced, (tsaw-baw), Strong's #H6633
Pronounced, (tseb-aw-aw') Strong's #H6633

Tsaba worship is a very strategic worship. It is a serious type of worship that requires the worshiper to wait on God's appointed time of resolution. I guarantee that as you wait on God, in His time, He will show up in charge and in command.

Tsaba worship is the type of worship required, when you have exhausted all means of natural ability, and beseech the hand of God to defend, avenge and come to your rescue.

The Names of God in this type of worship:
- The Commander of the LORD's Army
- The Captain of the LORD GOD of Hosts
- The LORD GOD of Hosts
- The LORD of Hosts
- The King of Glory, The Lord God Strong and Mighty in Battle

Joshua worshiped the Commander of the LORD's Army before he fought the battle of Jericho. Read Joshua 5:13-15

1 Chronicles 17:24 - His Name, LORD of Hosts must be magnified.
Isaiah 44:6 – Besides Me there is no God.

When we worship the Captain of the LORD GOD of Hosts, we are literally bringing all of heaven's warfare and battle to work on our behalf.

As you wait upon God in Tsaba worship, you not only have The Captain of the LORD's Host with you, but also have:

- A mass of angelic hosts organized for war
- An army ready for battle
- Spiritual soldiers ready to fight on your behalf
- A host of heaven assembled to perform the Word of the Lord
- A company of angels ready to help those who are heir of salvation

Who are we referring to when we say, "hosts"?
The "hosts" are angels or celestial beings who God created as His servants. They are also called the sons of God, and Lucifer was created along with them. Job 1:6

Psalm 33:6
By the word of the LORD the heavens were made, and all the host of them by the breath of His mouth.

The Hosts of Heaven worships the LORD
Nehemiah 9:6
You alone are the LORD; You have made heaven, the heaven of heavens, with all their host, the earth and everything on it, the seas and all that is in them, and You preserve them all. The host of heaven worships You.

The Angels and Host excel in strength
Psalm 103:20-21

20) *Bless the LORD, you His angels, who excel in strength, who do His word, heeding the voice of His word.*

21) *Bless the LORD, all you His hosts, you ministers of His, who do His pleasure.*

The Angels and Hosts praise Him
Psalm 148:2

Praise Him, all His angels;
Praise Him, all His hosts!

The Hosts of Heaven are innumerable
Jeremiah 33:22

As the host of heaven cannot be numbered, so the sand of the sea.

Scriptures: Daniel 7:10; 1 Kings 22:19; Isaiah 13:1-4

God demands fear and reverence in Tsaba Worship
- He is greatly to be feared and reverenced. Psalm 89:7-8

God Gives Counsel and Guidance in Tsaba Worship
- He is great in counsel – Jeremiah 32:18-19;
- He is wonderful in counsel & guidance – Isaiah 28:29

The LORD of Hosts must be exalted in Tsaba Worship
- The proud and lofty will be humbled, but the Lord will be exalted. Isaiah 2:11-17

The LORD of Hosts is awesome
The LORD of Hosts is so awesome that His thoughts come to pass and whatever He purposes shall stand. Isaiah 14:24-27

The LORD of Hosts helped King David kill Goliath
1 Samuel 17:45
King David was a man of war, and he knew what it was like to have the Lord of Hosts fighting on his side. The Lord of Hosts can help kill your giants in Tsaba worship.

Tsaba Worship gives Spiritual Vision
Elisha was sought after by the Syrian army, but he was not afraid because he was a man of Tsaba worship. He told his servant this:

2 Kings 6:16
"So he answered, 'Do not fear, for those who are with us are more than those who are with them.'"

The invisible became visible, and God opened Elisha's eyes to the spiritual realm and he saw a host of horses and chariots of fire all around the mountain. Tsaba worship will open your eyes and allow you to see what others can't see!

The Lord of Hosts – Tsaba Worship
Jeremiah 28:2; Jeremiah 30:8 - Breaks yokes
Jeremiah 11:20 – He judges righteously & tries the hearts
Jeremiah 35:13 - He's a God of Instruction

Jeremiah 50:34 – Pleads your case and gives rest
Their Redeemer is strong; the LORD of hosts is His name. He will thoroughly plead their case, that He may give rest to the land, and disquiet the inhabitants of Babylon.

Note: He gives you rest, and gives your enemies unrest.

One important fact in this type of worship is that we must be careful to obey whatever the Lord says to us; as He is not only the God of war but also the God who corrects us when we are wrong, Jeremiah 44th chapter.

However, when you obey Him as the Lord of Hosts, you and the generations after you can stand before Him forever, Jeremiah the 35th chapter.

The Lord of Hosts – Tsaba Worship Brings Joy & gladness
Jeremiah 33:11
"The voice of joy and the voice of gladness, the voice of the bridegroom and the voice of the bride, the voice of those who will say: 'Praise the LORD of hosts, for the LORD is good, for His mercy endures forever.'"

Worship in Healing

Who Himself bore our sins in His own body on the tree, that we, having died to sins, might live for righteousness—by whose stripes you were healed.
1 Peter 2:24

God works through the medical profession in healing the sick; however, what happens when there is no cure? What happens when the doctor says nothing else can be done? What happens when you, yourself, have tried everything and nothing works, and your body writhes in pain and become tiresome and weak, thinking there is no hope? Where is hope and what is the answer? Can you believe that the answer is in worship?

Therapeuo Worship
Therapeuo, Greek #2323
Pronounced, (ther-ap-yoo'-o)

Facts about this worship:
- To wait on and adore God in worship to cure and heal
- To relieve of disease
- To restore health
- God tends, takes care of, and provides for the sick
- Waiting upon God for divine healing

Our English word, therapy, or therapeutic is derived from this word, therapeuo. Therapy means healing through the process of treatment, and rehabilitation. Therapy involves two (2) people; one who is giving the treatment and one who is receiving it. In this type of worship, Jesus is the One tending and caring, and we are the ones benefiting as we are restored to health.

Therapeuo worship is what we give to God as we love and wait upon Him; waiting upon God for divine healing, trusting and knowing that He is the only One that can relieve us of our disease and He is the only One that can cure our whole being; physically, mentally, and emotionally.

For I will restore health to you
And heal you of your wounds, says the LORD.
Jeremiah 30:17

Waiting on our Healer – Jehovah Rapha

Jehovah Rapha; we've studied about this redemptive name in the earlier chapter, Praise and the Redemptive Names of God; however, the following is a further explanation of the word, rapha:

Rapha, Hebrew, #7495
- To mend by stitching
- To cure
- To heal
- Physician
- To repair
- Thoroughly make whole

Jehovah Rapha not only heals our bodies, but He heals our minds; He heals how we think, how we feel, and how we respond. He's concerned about the whole totality of man; spirit, soul, and body

Jesus – The Sun of Righteousness

But to you who fear My name The Sun of Righteousness shall arise
with healing in His wings;
Malachi 4:2

Jesus, the Great Physician, is like the brilliant sun coming out of its chamber, rising with the morning rays of hope. He is The Healer of Righteousness defending the side of justice, and moral virtue. His powerful beam sends forth emission of light to illuminate the pain of darkness hidden deep inside our psyche. We are wholesome and sound; restored to tranquility; the entire person is completely repaired.

Healing in His Wings
The word, "healing", is the Hebrew #4832, "<u>marpe</u>" (pronounced "mar-pay"), which means, medicine, deliverance, remedy, curative. In addition, the word, "wings" is "<u>kanaph</u>", Hebrew #3671, which means an edge, or extremity of a garment; a border, corner, or flap of a garment. Study on this is actually <u>referring to a prayer shawl</u>.

A Woman Experiences Physical Healing
Luke 8:43, 44, 47

The woman with the issue of blood knew that Jesus had healing in His wings; Jesus was wearing a prayer shawl; a Tallith.
43) Now a woman, having a flow of blood for twelve years, who had spent all her livelihood on physicians and could not be healed by any, 44) came from behind and touched the border of His garment. And immediately her flow of blood stopped.

Luke 8:47
"Now when the woman saw that she was not hidden, she came trembling; and <u>falling down before Him,</u> she declared to Him in the presence of all the people the reason she had touched Him and how she was healed immediately."

A Demon-Possessed Man Experiences Mental Healing
Luke 8:26-39

Jesus not only healed those with physical ailments, but also mental sickness, as we see in the story of a man from the country of Gadarenes.

This man had demons for a long time and wore no clothes. The scriptures describe him as not living in a house, but among tombs, which certainly did not allow him the capability of living a normal life.

Because of this condition, the man had to be kept under guard. Ultimately he would break free of the chains and shackles and hide in the wilderness. However, when he encountered Jesus, the Son of God, he was delivered from this torment, and the Bible says he was in his right mind.

Luke 8:35-36
35) Then they went out to see what had happened, and came to Jesus, and found the man from whom the demons had departed, sitting at the feet of Jesus, clothed and in his right mind. And they were afraid.
36) They also who had seen it told them by what means he who had been demon-possessed was healed.

The word, "healed" in the scripture, is the word, "sozo", #H4982, which means to save, heal, and to deliver.

Those who are demon-possessed or have mental illnesses are victimized by fear and a lack of love. This fear harnesses the feelings of the mind, the understanding, and the cognitive faculties, disallowing them to make right choices and wise decisions. This is not just any type of fear (as in being afraid of flying); this is a strengthened form of fear (a stronghold) that fences in and encloses the mind to block up and silence a sound mind.

This type of fear immobilizes and torments its victims, making them feel hopeless and powerless, and the mind is conditioned to believe all types of lies and phobias. A person of this nature is in awe of the fear more than the awe and reverence of God.

The Bible says that God has not given us a mental disposition of timidity or fear; why? Because God's agape love (which is unconditional) has been poured out in our hearts by the Holy Spirit, and this love brings fulfillment (Romans 5:5). This agape love reveals to us that we are loved no matter what, and upon receiving this love, we learn how to give love..........to be loved, and to love.

The mental disposition that God gives is one of mighty ability, good judgment, and of self-disciplined thought patterns. It is one that has the ability to understand and make right decisions, and exhibit the qualities of self-discipline and self-control. Therefore, as one practice to love and be loved, he or she is complete and need never to fear, because he or she has the soundness of God's love surrounding them— God's love and the love of others. The thought process of being loved is the initial process of healing. It is the love factor, as well as help from others, such as counseling and healthy interactions that bring about this change.
2 Timothy 1:7 and 1 John 4:18.

Jesus is Called the Dayspring From on High
He is called the Dayspring From on High, who has visited us; to give light to those who sit in darkness and in the shadow of death, to guide our feet into the way of peace. Luke 1:78-79

Isaiah 9:2
"The people who walked in darkness have seen a great light; those who dwelt in the land of the shadow of death, upon them a light has shined."

Jesus was Anointed by God to do Good and to Heal
Acts 10:38
"How God anointed Jesus of Nazareth with the Holy Spirit and with power, who went about doing good and healing all who were oppressed by the devil, for God was with Him."

EXAMPLES OF HEALING

Many multitudes of people waited on Jesus as He would go from city to city preaching, teaching, and healing.

Example #1
Luke 8:40-56

- As the multitude was waiting on Jesus, a man came and worshiped Jesus and begged Him to come and heal his daughter.

Luke 8:40

"So it was, when Jesus returned, that the multitude welcomed Him, for they were all <u>waiting</u> on Him."

Verse 40 says they were all waiting on Him, however, pay close attention to what they were doing while they were waiting: <u>worshipping</u>. Jairus fell down at Jesus' feet. Remember, kneeling is a form of Shachah worship.

Luke 8:41

"And behold, there came a man named Jairus, and he was a ruler of the synagogue. And <u>he fell down at Jesus' feet</u> and begged Him to come to his house."

Example #2
John 5:1-16
Again, Jesus is going to the place of the sick, and this time it is at the Pool of Bethesda.

John 5:3

"In these lay a great multitude of sick people, blind, lame, paralyzed, <u>waiting</u> for the moving of the water."

These people were waiting for an angel to stir up the water and the first person who stepped in the water was healed, but in walks Jesus

161

Christ, the Son of God, who is Jehovah Rapha, and He has mercy on a man that couldn't get to the pool fast enough to be healed.

Jesus says to him, "Do you want to be made well?" "Rise, take up your bed and walk."

The command to this man was to rise and take up his bed and walk; however, in some instances, healing may not come immediately. In therapy, a doctor may give a list of things to do while in the process of being healed. The _therapy_ in therapeuo worship is simply this: _loving and worshiping God._ While you're waiting, God in His sovereignty may heal you immediately or give wisdom (treatment or remedies) on what _you_ should do to bring about healing.

The Bible says that we are partakers of His Divine Nature. This means that we participate with God's divine power by believing in His precious promises to bring about life and godliness. 2 Peter 1:3-4.

2 Kings 5:10-14
In the Old Testament, Naaman, the Leper was told to dip 7 times in the Jordan River and he would be healed of his leprosy. Naaman didn't want to do this at first because the river was not as clean as the others, but when he did; his skin was <u>clean as a baby's skin.</u>

Mark 3:1-5
Jesus instructed the man with the withered hand to:
1) Step forward
2) Stretch out your hand

Mark 8:22-26 - Gradual Healing
- Jesus gradually heals a blind man:
- Took the blind man by the hand
- Took him out of the town
- Spit on his eyes (the man didn't see clearly at first)

- Told him to look up
- Put His hands on the man's eyes again
- The blind man was restored and saw everyone clearly.

Jesus is willing to heal

It is Jesus' will to heal and take care of the sick. In Matthew 8:1-3, the leper says to Jesus, "Lord, if You are willing, You can make me clean." Jesus says, "I am willing; be cleansed." In Matthew 8:5-13, after the Centurion pleads with Jesus to come and heal his servant, Jesus says, "I will come and heal him."

Jesus heals various sick people
Matthew 4:23-24

23) And Jesus went about all Galilee, teaching in their synagogues, preaching the gospel of the kingdom and healing all kinds of sickness and all kinds of disease among the people.
24) Then His fame went throughout all Syria; and they brought to Him all sick people who were afflicted with various diseases and torments, and those who were demon-possessed, epileptics, and paralytics; and He healed them.

Luke 9:1

Jesus gave the disciples the authority to heal in His name.

Mark 16:15-18

Jesus, in the Great Commission, gives us authority to heal in His Name.

Therapeuo Worship requires putting away all dishonor and unbelief
Mark 6:1-6

Dishonor and unbelief limits Jesus' ability from doing the mighty works of healing; for the Bible says in Mark 6:5 that He only could heal a few sick people.

It is also noted that Jesus, being a prophet, was not honored amongst His own kinfolk, and because of dishonor, the spirit of unbelief spread quickly. In fact, He marveled so much at their unbelief that instead of healing, He went about the village teaching. It is not expressed what was being taught, but I can only imagine Jesus teaching on how to receive healing. Selah.

Jesus is the Balm of Gilead - Jeremiah 8:22
"Is there no balm in Gilead, is there no physician there? Why then is there no recovery for the health of the daughter of my people?"

People traveled to the city of Gilead for resources of balms, cures and to be seen of physicians. Jesus is the Balm of Gilead who brings recovery of health to His people through Therapeuo worship!

Amen!

WORSHIP IN OFFERINGS

Giving is a true form of worship. Giving is what God did when He gave His only begotten Son.

For God so loved the world that He gave His only begotten son that whoever believes in Him should not perish, but have everlasting life.
John 3:16

You may ask, "What does giving have to do with worship?"

God gave out of love, and He gave His firstfruit, which was His Son, to obtain more sons (that's us). When giving tithes and offerings, our attitude should be one of worship, honor, love, respect, humility, and obedience. The Children of Israel also worshiped the Lord through giving:

Deuteronomy 26:10
"And now behold, I have brought the firstfruits of the land which you, O LORD have given me. Then you shall set it before the LORD your God, and worship the LORD your God."

II Chronicles 29:29
"And when they had finished offering, the King and all who were present with him bowed and worshiped."

Giving to God is very sacred. It is not all about money, but the giving of ourselves to Him. This is worship and God is well pleased.

Mark 10:17-22 describes a person who did not worship God in giving. Yes, he is called, the Rich Young Ruler. When this Ruler first encountered Jesus, we find that he has a heart for worship because he runs to Jesus and kneels before him; however, his worship is subdued by something Jesus asked him to do.

Jesus loved this Ruler because he kept the commandments, and he was very eager about inheriting eternal life. He had all the requirements to be a follower of Jesus Christ. Nonetheless, Jesus says to him, "One thing you lack". I'm sure he had everything; what could possibly be lacking from his life? He was lacking in giving; not only giving of money, but giving himself to God. When Jesus told the Ruler to sell all he had and give to the poor, he went away saddened and grieved. In actuality, Jesus was giving him an opportunity of a lifetime to become a disciple. This opportunity passed him by because the Ruler's trust was not in Jesus, but in riches; his riches ruled him.

What about us today? Can we worship God in our giving, no matter what the cost? Can we leave our riches and take up our cross and follow Jesus? Selah; pause and think of that.

As worshipers, our motive in giving is that we love God and we honor Him with our possessions,

Proverbs 3:9-10
9) Honor the LORD with your possessions, and with the firstfruits of all your increase;
10) So your barns will be filled with plenty, and your vats will overflow with new wine.

As we worship God in tithes and offerings, God promises that the windows of heaven are opened, and blessing is poured out to us, not only that, but the devourer is rebuked and our vine shall not fail to bear fruit. What a blessing!

Malachi 3:10-11
10) "Bring all the tithes into the storehouse, that there may be food in My house, and try Me now in this," *says the LORD of hosts,* "If I will not open for you the windows of heaven and pour out for you such blessing that there will not be room enough to receive it.

11) And I will rebuke the devourer for your sakes, so that he will not destroy the fruit of your ground, nor shall the vine fail to bear fruit for you in the field," says the LORD of hosts.

Let us make the decision to follow Christ and not riches; this truly is an act of worship.

WORSHIP IS IN YOUR FUTURE

I am not well versed in prophecy, but one thing is certain: WORSHIP IS IN YOUR FUTURE and it would be a good idea to start practicing "worship" while you are here on this earth. Zechariah 14:16-18 explains that in the end times, we will come to Jerusalem to worship:

16) And it shall come to pass that everyone who is left of all the nations which came against Jerusalem shall go up from year to year to worship the King, the LORD of hosts, and to keep the Feast of Tabernacles.

17) And it shall be that whichever the families of the earth do not come up to Jerusalem to worship the King, the LORD of hosts, on them there will be no rain.

18) If the family of Egypt will not come up and enter in, they shall have no rain; they shall receive the plague with which the LORD strikes the nations who do not come up to keep the Feast of Tabernacles.

Did you notice verse 17 states that if they did not come to worship, there would be no rain? I don't know if this is symbolic or literal rain, but in any case, we can certainly say that when we worship God, it is like a refreshing rain falling down from Heaven that makes the situation in our lives become productive, and our personal lives fruitful. However, when there is no worship, we will experience a plague. A plague might be a financial hardship, or it may be a broken relationship. Whatever it may be, God can make the crooked way straight as we return to worship.

Again, we read about the tribulation saints in Revelation 15:1-4, 8 which states:

1) "Then I saw another sign in Heaven, great and marvelous: seven angles having the seven last plagues, for in them the wrath of God is complete.

2) And I saw something like a sea of glass mingled with fire, and those who have the victory over the beast, over his image and over his mark and over the number of his name, standing on the sea of glass, having harps of God.

3) They sing the song of Moses, the servant of God, and the song of the Lamb, saying: 'Great and marvelous are Your works, Lord God Almighty! Just and true are Your ways, O King of the saints.

4) Who shall not fear You, O Lord, and glorify Your name? For You alone are holy. For all nations shall come and worship before You. For Your judgments have been manifested'."

8) The temple was filled with smoke from the glory of God and from His power, and no one was able to enter the temple till the seven plagues of the seven angels were completed."

What a magnificent picture of God's glory manifested through singing a song! We can also find the song of Moses in Exodus 15:1-21, and another song in Deuteronomy 32:1-43. These songs talk about victory and deliverance. In Moses' time, it was a song of victory and deliverance over Pharaoh, but in the coming age, it will be a song of victory and deliverance over the Antichrist. We also previously talked about the Song of the Lamb, which is in Revelation 5:8-14.

WHOM WILL YOU WORSHIP?

Worship will play an important role in the great tribulation.........."IF" you are here, whom will you worship? Will you worship Christ? If so, it will cost your very life in martyrdom, but you will live with Christ throughout eternity. Will you worship the antichrist? If so, you'll be doomed to eternal hell.

Revelation 13:12

And he exercises all the authority of the first beast in his presence, and causes the earth and those who dwell in it to worship the first beast, whose deadly wound was healed.

Why not make the decision to worship the King now? You won't regret it!

The Song of Worship
(A Song of the Redeemed)

As born-again believers, we have been given the awesome privilege of learning a new song that no one else can sing. It's a song of joyful celebration that we have been redeemed by the Blood of the Lamb. It's a song of restoration drawing us back to a peaceful relationship with God, and it's the song of salvation that God's Beloved Son, who sits at His right hand, has brought forth victory!

Psalm 98:1, 2, 4
1) OH, sing to the LORD a new song! For He has done marvelous things; His right hand and His holy arm have gained Him the victory.
2) The LORD has made known His salvation; His righteousness He has revealed in the sight of the nations.
4) Shout joyfully to the LORD, all the earth; break forth in song, rejoice, and sing praises.

Psalm 96:1-2
1) OH, sing to the LORD a new song! Sing to the LORD, all the earth.
2) Sing to the LORD, bless His name; Proclaim the good news of His salvation from day to day.

The conclusion of the whole matter is this: Singing is very important to God. It is expressed throughout the entire Bible we read. Let us always take time to remember that what is important to God should also be important to us.

Amen!

Preaching to the Choir

Our responsibility as a choir of worshipers is to have a heart of worship toward God first and foremost. Therefore, since you have the heart of worship, the congregation can engage in worship as well, and everyone is blessed by the Presence of God.

There can never be enough said about worship; the following are a few other things that a choir member can meditate on in preparation for worship.

WORSHIP is obedience to God's Word and God's Will. Jesus gave us a true example of worship when He was in the Garden of Gethsemane. His spirit was distressed about going to the cross, but His words were, "Not My will, Father, but Thine will be done. (Luke 22:42). When we enter into worship with the Father, we may, like Jesus, be stressed to the limit, but as we spend time before Him, He will change our lives to be conformed to His will. It will not be comfortable, but it will be necessary.

WORSHIP is giving of oneself to God. Jesus exemplified giving of oneself as He was dying on the cross. He said these words, "Father, into your hands I commit my spirit." (Luke 23:46). Daily we should ask ourselves, "Have I committed my life to God?" Also ask, "Is there anything that I haven't given to you, Heavenly Father? Please reveal this to me, that I might give my whole life to You."

What is the difference between praise and worship?
Praise is the expressed glorification of God. Praise expresses what He has done. Worship expresses adoration, love, and the exaltation of God. Worship is all about God, and as participants of worship, our role is to express reverence and submission to God. As stated before, the real expression of worship is a total surrendered life of obedience to God.

How do you express worship?

As we know, God is looking at our heart at all times, but there are ways in which we can express worship through our body language, and through our words. We find many scriptures where bowing and kneeling to the Lord is common. Psalm 141:2 is actually referring to prayer, but it is my favorite scripture in reference to lifting our hands:

- *Let my prayer be set before You as incense, the lifting up of my hands as the evening sacrifice.*

In Numbers 28:1-8, two lambs were sacrificed daily by the priests; one as the morning sacrifice, and one as the evening sacrifice. But now, since Jesus Christ was, and is the Lamb of God, He is the ultimate sacrifice, and we use the lifting of our hands as a sacrifice of our lives to Him. Read these scriptures also: Psalm 95:6, Psalm 28:2, and 1 Timothy 2:8.

EXPRESSIONS OF WORSHIP

When a rightly spoken word enter your ears, the results can be very pleasing. God, The Father, is the Author of the spoken Word. In Genesis, we find that God created the existing world with His Word. Words, even spoken negatively can cause an effect.

Throughout the Bible, there are particular words that when spoken change the atmosphere so that God's power and His presence are reality. Keep in mind that God's Presence does not need to be summoned like a genie in a bottle. The Bible says He is with us always, even unto the end of the world. We worship him for His Omnipresence; which means He is anywhere and everywhere. However, His Power is frequently demonstrated through praise and worship.

Revelation 4:8-11 is the ultimate scene of worship. Here we find that the four Living Creatures and the twenty-four elders are saying words that capture the true essence of worship:

Revelation 4:8

"The four living creatures, each having six wings, were full of eyes around and within. And they do not rest day or night, saying:
   'Holy, holy, holy
   Lord God Almighty,
   Who was and is and is to come!'

9) The living creatures give glory and honor and thanks to Him who sits on the throne, who lives forever and ever,

10) The twenty-four elders fall down before Him who sits on the throne and worship Him who lives forever and ever, and cast their crowns before the throne, saying:

11) 'You are worthy, O Lord,
   To receive glory and honor and power;
   For You created all things,
   And by Your will they exist and
   Were created'."

The central theme of worship is the Lord God Almighty, and to Him ascribed glory, honor, and power through words being spoken. These exact words can be applied to our own daily devotionals. A praise and worship leader can speak these words to invoke the presence of God during praise and worship service.

Here is another example of Expressions of Worship:

Revelation 5:9-14

9) "And they sang a new song, saying:
   'You are worthy to take the scroll,
   And to open its seals;
   For You were slain,
   And have redeemed us to God by

Your blood
Out of every tribe and tongue and
People and nation,

10) And have made us kings and priests to our God;
   And we shall reign on the earth.'

11) Then I looked, and I heard the voice of many angels around the throne,
   the living creatures, and the elders; and the number of them was
   ten thousand times ten thousand, and thousands of thousands,

12) Saying with a <u>LOUD VOICE</u>:
   'Worthy is the Lamb who was slain
   To receive power and riches and wisdom,
   And strength and honor and glory and blessing!'

13) And every creature which is in heaven and on the earth and under the
   Earth and such as are in the sea, and all that are in them, I heard saying:
   'Blessing and honor and glory and power
   Be to Him who sits on the throne,
   And to the Lamb, forever, and ever!'

14) Then the four living creatures said, 'Amen!' And the twenty-four elders fell down and worshiped Him who lives forever and ever."

WOW! In addition to the Awesomeness of God, we also see the Worthiness of the Lamb of God, who is Jesus Christ. We must say, "Selah" right now.

WORDS OF EXALTATION

As God is the author and true source of our worship, we exalt Him in all His glory.

1 Chronicles 29:10-12

"Blessed are You, LORD God of Israel our Father, forever and ever. Yours, O LORD, is the greatness, the power and the glory, the victory and the majesty; For all that is in heaven and in earth is Yours; Yours is the kingdom, O LORD, and You are exalted as head over all. Both riches and honor come from You, and You reign over all. In Your hand is power and might; In Your hand it is to make great and to give strength to all." (NKJV)

In this scripture, David had just finished collecting an offering for the building of the Temple. The people of God had given with a willing heart, and David so eloquently expresses glory and exaltation to God. Some of these words are repeated in the New Testament from the Lord's Prayer.........For Thine is the kingdom, the power and the glory. What better way to make our prayer known to God than to glorify and exalt Him in every situation, whether in sickness or disease, poverty or lack, oppression or depression; we can go on and on. I challenge you to try this in your daily prayer; you will never be the same.

MORE LANGUAGE OF EXALTATION
Psalm 86:8-10

"Among the gods there is none like You, O Lord; nor are there any works like Your works. All nations whom You have made shall come and worship before You, O Lord, and shall glorify Your name. For You are great, and do wondrous things; You alone are God." (NKJV)

In this Psalm, David is praying for mercy while at the same time, he exalts God.

Let's break it down:

- EXALTATION – *Among the gods there is none like you, O Lord.*
- EXALTING HIS WORKS – *Nor are there any works like Your works.*
- ACKNOWLEDGMENT, GLORIFICATION – *All nations whom You have made shall come and worship before You, O Lord.*
- EXALTATION – *For You are great, and do wondrous things. You alone are God.*

Hosea 11:7 is another scripture that describes exaltation; however, it speaks of it as a reprimand because the people didn't exalt Him.

Part B of the scripture says:
............*Though they call to the Most High, none at all exalt Him.*

Let us be ever so careful not only to call on the Lord with mere words, but also let us exalt Him with a sincere heart in every situation.

CHAPTER 8

When God Won't Hear Your Song. . .

Amos 5:1-27

Have you ever given thought to the fact that God will not accept your song of praise? This is a hard statement to accept; however, we find it clearly expressed in the Bible. Have I gotten your attention? One thing that I find prevalent in reading the Word of God: Almighty God is a God of justice, and He does not take injustice or unrighteousness lightly.

In the fifth chapter of Amos and the 23rd verse, God relays a message to the Children of Israel: "Take away from Me the noise of your songs, for I will not hear the melody of your stringed instruments." Verse 24 says, "But let justice run down like water, and righteousness like a mighty stream." What was this about? Amos considered that Israel is forsaken, and she will not rise again. He considered her dead; therefore, this chapter is a song of lament, or a funeral song.

Ironically, God uses a song of lament to express to Israel that He will not hear their song. Why would God make such a statement? This was not the time for a song of praise and worship; it was a time for repentance. The state of Israel was idolatry and oppression of the poor. All

God wanted from them was to seek Him and live; forsake the idols, forsake evil; do good, and establish justice.

The Living Bible translation:

23) "Away with your hymns of praise---they are mere noise to My ears. I will not listen to your music, no matter how lovely it is.
24) "I want to see a mighty flood of justice---a torrent of doing good.

How much clearer can God be? Can it be that God does not accept our praise and worship in the midst of injustice and unrighteousness? The answer is a resounding, YES! Verse 23 says their praise and worship was mere noise. Why? They delighted in sacrificial offerings and "public worship" and neglected the weightier matters----righteousness and justice. As a result of this behavior, their ultimate punishment is to be exiled from the land that was promised to Abraham, Isaac, and Jacob. And according to verses 25 and 26, not only were they worshipers of God, but also worshipers of their pagan gods, Sakkuth and Kaiwan. This thing ought not to be!

God loves to bless His people, however, blessings are conditioned based on our response and obedience to what is being communicated. How we treat others will affect our praise and worship to God. Amos 5 should challenge us to "step-it-up" in our relationship with God and man. The bottom line is this: Seek God, forsake evil, and align our lives with justice and righteousness; then God will accept our praise and worship.

CHAPTER **9**

Glory in the Congregation

And Moses was not able to enter the tabernacle of meeting,
because the cloud rested above it, and the glory of the LORD
filled the tabernacle.
Exodus 40:35

THE SHEKINAH GLORY OF GOD

In the Old Testament, the Presence of God could be seen by what was called the Glory of God, the Glory of the LORD, or the Glory Cloud. What exactly is this?

As mentioned in the earlier chapters, the Glory of the LORD is the Kabad of the Lord, which describes God as glorious and very great in splendor and majesty. It is God's glory that is very great and weighty; numerous, rich and honorable.

The Glory Cloud represented an expression of God that the Children of Israel could actually see; for it was a pillar of cloud by day and a pillar of fire by night.

The Glory Cloud was also a significant representation of God's approval. We see this exemplified when Moses finished the work of the tabernacle, and the Glory of the LORD appeared.

Exodus 40:33-34

33) "And he raised up the court all around the tabernacle and the altar, and hung up the screen of the court gate. So Moses finished the work.
34) Then the cloud covered the tabernacle of meeting, and the Glory of the LORD filled the tabernacle."

ANOTHER EXAMPLE OF GOD'S GLORY

King Solomon finished building the Temple and as a dedication, rendered a beautiful prayer unto the Lord. Upon approval, God's glory is once again physically seen and fills the Temple.

2 Chronicles 7:1-3

1) "When Solomon had finished praying, fire came down from heaven and consumed the burnt offering and the sacrifices; and the glory of the LORD filled the temple.
2) And the priests could not enter the house of the LORD, because the glory of the LORD had filled the LORD's house.
3) When all the children of Israel saw how the fire came down, and the glory of the LORD on the temple, they bowed their faces to the ground on the pavement, and worshiped and praised the LORD, saying:

'For He is good, for His mercy endures forever.'"

God's Glory is His Goodness
Exodus 33:12-23

The Lord spoke to Moses face to face, as a man speaks to his friend. Through experience, Moses has seen God's mighty power demonstrated by delivering the Jews from the hand of Pharaoh. However, this time, Moses wanted something more than God's Presence; he wanted to see God's glory.

His conversation with the Lord is very unique; for he says,

Exodus 33:13

13) "Now therefore, I pray, if I have found grace in Your sight, show me now Your way, that I may know You and that I may find grace in Your sight. And consider that this nation is Your people."

Pay close attention to the words, "Show me now Your way, that I may know You". The words "show" and "know" have the same meaning: Yada; we've studied this word previously; it means to know intimately.

In today's vernacular, Moses is saying, "If I have favor with You, show me how I can know You; I want to see who You really are, I want to intimately know all about Your thoughts and Your whole self."

To culminate his ultimate request, Moses makes this astounding statement:

Exodus 33:18

And he said, "Please, show me Your glory."

From a final thought, Moses is saying,

"I want to gaze upon Your Plenteous Goodness"

God answers Moses so beautifully:

Exodus 33:19

"Then He said, 'I will make all My goodness pass before you, and I will proclaim the name of the LORD before you. I will be gracious to whom I will be gracious, and I will have compassion on whom I will have compassion'."

God says to Moses, "I will make **all** My goodness pass before you.........

181

What is God's goodness?

Goodness – (Hebrew #2898) – Tub
Pronounced (toob)
- Beauty
- Gladness
- Welfare
- Joy
- Go well with

God's goodness is beautiful; God's goodness is joyful; God's goodness is gladness and well being; happiness, and safety. God's goodness is when things go well with you.

In other words, God says to Moses, "I'm not going to show you part of Me, but I'm going to show you **_all of My goodness_**." And guess what? Not only does God speak about His _goodness_, but He takes it further and talks about His _graciousness_ - "I will proclaim My name before you, and will be _gracious_, to whomever I will."

What is God's graciousness? "I will grant you _favor_ and show love, compassion, and mercy to whomever I will."

God prepares Moses to see His splendor by saying: "Here is a place by Me."

Exodus 33:21-22
21) "And the LORD said, 'Here is a place by Me, and you shall stand on the rock.
22) So it shall be, while My glory passes by, that I will put you in the cleft of the rock, and will cover you with My hand while I pass by.'"

Worshiper of God, wouldn't you love to hear God say: "Here is a place by Me; My glory, My goodness, and My graciousness will pass by you?" Wow!!!!

So God says to Moses, "So be ready in the morning......" Exodus 34:2

There is something about spending time in the morning with God. It's like fresh dew on the morning grass.........so refreshing.

MOSES BEHOLDS GOD'S GOODNESS
Exodus 34:5-8
Moses finally gets to gaze upon God's Goodness as he sees the Glory Cloud descending, and a proclamation was heard:

Exodus 34:6-7
6) "And the LORD passed before him and proclaimed, 'The LORD, the LORD God, merciful and gracious, longsuffering, and abounding in goodness and truth,
7) keeping mercy for thousands, forgiving iniquity and transgression and sin, by no means clearing the guilty, visiting the iniquity of the fathers upon the children and the children's children to the third and the fourth generation.'"

In this proclamation is the knowledge of God and in the study of all the Hebrew words and so forth, I came to this conclusion of who God is:

The LORD, the LORD God, meaning, Jehovah, Jehovah is the Self-Existing God who is Eternal. He is God who is Strength and Mighty, Almighty and Goodly; Great and Powerful and Strong. At the same time, He is merciful and compassionate; He is gracious and patient, slow to anger, and passionately longsuffering. He is abundant in quantity and often in goodness, showing His kindness and favor by His good deeds toward man. He has pity, and lovingkindness; He guards, protects, and maintains mercy for a thousand generations to those who love Him; His mercies never end. His truth is His stability; He is faithful and establishes trustworthiness.

He forgives by lifting, carrying away, or casting away our sins. He forgives our faults, rebellion, and our habitual sinfulness. At the same time, He accepts, advances, and desires to help, hold up, and spare, and by no means will He clear the guilty, but will appoint punishment to those who sin, surely with no exception.

At this point, Moses could do nothing except worship.

WE MUST ASCRIBE GLORY TO GOD

In the New Testament there is also a "<u>glory</u>" that I do not say is actually seen, but a glory that is attributed to God in praise and worship. This glory is called, "doxa". This is taken from our English word, "Doxology"

<u>Doxa</u>, (Strong's Concordance, Greek, #1391)
Pronounced (dox-ah)
- Dignity
- Glory
- Honor
- Praise
- Worship

<u>Doxology:</u>
In Christian worship, a hymn in praise of the Almighty; a particular form of giving glory to God.

It is this type of glory that should be presented in our congregations—glory ascribed unto God! To Him and Him alone should be the attentiveness of our praise! No flesh shall glory in His Presence;

all dignity, glory, honor, praise, and worship belong to God, that He may be glorified and no one else!

The Apostle Peter says it this way:

To Him be glory and dominion for ever and ever. Amen.
1 Peter 5:11

Jude says it this way:

Now unto Him who is able to keep you from falling, and to present you faultless before the presence of His Glory, with exceeding joy

To the only wise God our Savior, be glory and majesty, domin-ion and power, both now and ever. Amen.

Jude 1:24-25

The same Glory that Moses experienced on the day when he said, "Show me Your Glory", is the same Glory that we can experience to-day. The Bible says *Jesus Christ, the same yesterday, today and forever!*

As we concentrate on the goodness of God, His brilliance will be powerful and His Glory will be evident. Most importantly, the con-gregation will be blessed and satiated by His Presence........... To save, to heal, to deliver, and to set free, and most of all, _there will be Glory in the Congregation!_

Isaiah 60:1
Arise, shine;
For your light has come!
And the glory of the LORD is risen upon you.

185

Isaiah 60:19

The sun shall no longer be your light by day,
Nor for brightness shall the moon give
Light to you;
But the LORD will be to you an
Everlasting light,
And your God your glory.

CHAPTER **10**

Preaching to the Choir
The Preparation

Anyone involved in praise and worship must realize that quality time spent with God is a requirement. Spending time in worship is a key ingredient. When we spend time in worship, we allow God to conform us to His will, His mind, and His heart. As we do this, God will begin to cleanse our hearts and effectively use us in the Praise and Worship service.

When a king was inaugurated in his kingdom, whatever was first implemented laid the foundation for whether it would be successful or not.

2 Chronicles 29:3-5 and 16 describes the acts of King Hezekiah when he first began to reign over Israel. The first thing he did was to restore worship into the temple. This is what he did:

- He opened the doors of the house of the Lord.
- He brought in the priest and Levites as was ordered by David.
- He **commanded** the Levites to sanctify themselves, and the house of the Lord.

We should practice the same thing as we prepare for praise and worship:

- Open our hearts to the Lord – <u>confession</u> and <u>repentance</u>.
- Have order in our hearts – put the <u>Word of God</u> first place in our hearts.
- Sanctify our hearts to the Lord – set apart our hearts to the Lord.

2 Chronicles 29:16 specifically shows us what to do:

- Go to the inner part of the house – <u>deep inside your heart</u>.
- Bring out all uncleanness – <u>sins</u>
- Carry it out to the brook – <u>get rid of it</u>!

This is a time for you to be honest with yourself, and true to God. Allow the Holy Spirit to reveal to you what needs to be corrected, confessed, and repented in your life. Allow the Blood of Jesus to cleanse you from all unrighteousness, and be determined to live a life of a follower of Christ.

This whole process cleanses your heart, and it brings healing to your mind and your body. You will begin to be free from the conditions of your heart, and be <u>FREE TO PRAISE THE LORD!</u>

I cannot emphasize enough how important preparation is to God. After you sense the call of God on your life, He gives you the ability and might to do it; preparation is part of this ability.

As a praise and worship leader, what is done behind closed doors is sometimes revealed to the congregation. They will either see your excellence or your mistakes. Ministering to God in the inner court (worship) must be first place in your life.

In Ezekiel 44, there were certain Levites who were involved in idolatry, and they caused Israel to fall into iniquity because of their actions.

As a result of this, God said that these Levites could not come near Him to minister. What they did affected the children of Israel (the congregation).

Ezekiel 44:13
"And they shall not come near Me to minister to Me as priest, nor come near any of My Holy things, nor into the Most Holy place; but they shall bear their shame and their abominations which they have committed."

However, there were certain sects of priests and Levites, from the sons of Zadok, who kept charge of the sanctuary and were faithful to God. By their actions, they were able to go into the inner courts and minister unto God in the inner court, and minister to the people in the outer court. Read Ezekiel 44:15-19.

Ezekiel 44:15
"'But the priests , the Levites, the sons of Zadok, who kept charge of My sanctuary when the children of Israel went astray from Me, they shall come near Me to minister to Me; and they shall stand before Me to offer to Me the fat and the blood,' says the LORD GOD."

Now of course, we have to remember that this is the Old Testament, and the Blood of Jesus was not shed at this time; however, we as praise and worship leaders must realize the importance of living a holy life in our homes, on our jobs, and anywhere else. When we enter into worship to minister to God's people, we do not want to be an obstacle that prevents the Presence of God from being among the congregation.

How can you, as a worshiper find ways of preparation?

Prepare Spiritually
- Spend *quality time waiting* before His Presence –

- » Loving God
- » Pleasing God
- » Living a submitted life to God
- Have your own personal praise and worship service before going to church by listening to inspirational praise and worship songs.

Prepare Skillfully
- Eat right, and drink lots of water to hydrate your vocal cords.
- Listen and practice with vocal tapes to warm up your voice.
- Know and understand your voice range (alto, soprano, tenor)
- Know and understand your instrument (Piano, flute, percussion)

You, who are the Royal Priesthood, are chosen to <u>Proclaim the Praises</u> of Him who called you out of darkness into His marvelous light!

1 Peter 2:9

Preaching to the Choir
(To the Minister of Music)

Operation Burn-Out
(Outer Court Process – Inner Court Renewal)

Working in the ministry can be very exciting; our spirits soar; we are charged; we can run through hoops; we can bend a bow of steel, and we can run like Elijah, who outran chariots. Sometimes we accept this call of God with opened arms and work like the sun never goes down, gladly knowing that we are being effective for the Kingdom of God. At other times, if we're not careful, we are prone to become sick, betrayed, hurt, misunderstood; in pain, busted and disgusted, all for the cause of Christ; right?

Experiencing "burn-out" in the ministry can be easily done if we are not focused on the true essence of righteousness and the mission and purposes of our calling. But remember this; whenever we experience burn-out we can come to God in what I call the Outer Court Process to be healed so that we can minister in the Holy Place.

The Outer Court Process is simply this: Dwelling in the Presence of God in prayer in the Outer Court, and waiting there until He calls you to the Inner Court.

When we looked at the Tabernacle of Moses in the previous chapters, we saw that the Outer Court included the Brazen Altar and the Brazen Laver. Brazen is symbolic of judgment, and of course as we enter into His gates with thanksgiving and into His courts with praise, there is no need to receive judgment for our sins because the blood of Jesus has already taken care of that. However, when we experience burn-out, it is important that we stay at the place of sacrifice (Brazen Altar) and at the place of cleansing (Brazen Laver) to allow God to deal with our behaviors and issues.

In Leviticus 22:17-33, the LORD speaks to Moses in regards to the offerings or sacrifices that were considered accepted or of defect.

Leviticus 22:19-20
19) You shall offer of your own free will a male without blemish from the cattle, from the sheep, or from the goats.
20) Whatever has a defect, you shall not offer, for it shall not be acceptable on your behalf.
21) And whoever offers a sacrifice of a peace offering to the LORD, to fulfill his vow, or a freewill offering from the cattle or the sheep, it must be perfect to be accepted; there shall be no defect in it.

WHAT POINT AM I TRYING TO MAKE?

In the midst of ministry, are we an offering without blemish, leaning on the righteousness of Christ, or are we an offering that has a defect?

God says in Leviticus that He would not accept any offerings that were blind, broken or maimed, no ulcer, eczema or scabs. God says He didn't want to see any offerings with limbs too long or too short, bruised or crushed, torn or cut. (Leviticus 22:22-23)

If God didn't want that type of offering then, what makes us think that He wants this type of offering now? I'm speaking in particular to the offering of our lives. There may be times our lives are blinded from the truth; our hearts are broken and we become maimed; we get bruised by others, crushed and torn apart. In order to not have a burn-out, we must come to the Brazen Altar and Brazen Laver on a consistent basis so that the rivers of God can refresh us often.

Why would we set ourselves up to become defected? No one is perfect and we all have shortcomings.

One thing is for certain: As we approach the Brazen Altar, we are totally leaning on the righteousness of Jesus Christ, which will enable us to serve and minister at a much greater level than any human effort, as the Bible clearly notes that our own righteousness is as filthy rags. However, Jesus, the Lamb of God, was without blemish and without spot, 1 Peter 1:19

What is meant by an offering without blemish?

WITHOUT BLEMISH
Tamiym (taw-meem), Strong's #8549

This word first appears in Genesis 6:9: Noah was "perfect" in his generations. In Genesis 17:1, God tells Abram to walk before Him and be "blameless". Tamiym is also used to describe animals fit for sacrifice, without blemish. This word has to deal with being perfect and fit for use.

The root verb tamam (#8552) means "to finish, use up, accomplish, be spent, and be completed."

- Unblemished
- Perfect
- Complete
- Full
- Upright
- Sincere
- Spotless
- Whole
- Healthy
- Blameless

The above mentioned truly exemplifies a sacrifice. This is what we become in ministry; all used up, spent, and accomplished, and in the process of time we might become defected.

Ministry can sometime be cruel; ask Jesus when He was betrayed by Peter. Ask Paul when he talks about being a minister suffering for Christ, 2 Corinthians 11:22-33. This is a GOOD READ. Please read the entire verses in your devotion time.

2 Corinthians 11:23-24
23) Are they ministers of Christ? ---I speak as a fool----I am more: in labors more abundant, in stripes above measure, in prisons more frequently, in deaths often.
24) From the Jews five times I received forty stripes minus one.

What does this have to do with worship? Worship is key to revitalization.

OUTER COURT PROCESS

BRAZEN ALTAR
As we approach the Brazen Altar and acknowledge the Blood of Christ and receive the forgiveness of sins, let us also allow ourselves to be forgiven and not stay in condemnation, and allow ourselves to forgive others as we have been forgiven. Let us allow ourselves to love, as we are loved by God unconditionally, and allow others to love us.

This Outer Court Process is certainly a healing factor, and it is certainly worshiping God in spirit and truth, as we become truthful to God, truthful to ourselves, and truthful to others. This is WORSHIP!

In this process, we may need to remain, stay, dwell, park, spend the night; do whatever we have to do at the Brazen Altar until God is done with us. Further examine yourself: have I hurt others? Have others hurt me? Am I walking in faith? Am I portraying Christ? Whatever the issues are, deal with it! As an animal is sacrificed at the Brazen Altar, sacrifice and kill all negative emotions that would prevent you from ministering in the Holy Place.

BRAZEN LAVAR

Another Outer Court Process is dwelling at the Brazen Laver by being washed with the Water of the Word of God. The book of Ephesians tells us that Jesus Himself, sanctifies and cleanses us and we become His church, without spot or wrinkle; holy and without blemish.

Ephesians 5:26-27

26) so that He might sanctify and cleanse her with the washing of water by the word.

27) that He might present her to Himself a glorious church, not having spot or wrinkle or any such thing, but that she should be holy and without blemish.

Paul encourages us about the Marks of the Ministry, as he not only reveals the subject of suffering, but encourages us to commend ourselves as ministers of God:

2 Corinthians 6:1-10

1. We then, as workers together with Him also plead with you not to receive the grace of God in vain:
2. For He says: "In an acceptable time I have heard you, and in the day of salvation I have helped you."
3. We give no offense in anything, that our ministry may not be blamed.
4. But in all things we commend ourselves as ministers of God: in much patience, in tribulations, in needs, in distresses,
5. in stripes, in imprisonments, in tumults, in labors, in sleeplessness, in fastings;
6. by purity, by knowledge, by longsuffering, by kindness, by the Holy Spirit, by sincere love,
7. by the word of truth, by the power of God, by the armor of righteousness on the right hand and on the left,
8. by honor and dishonor, by evil report and good report; as deceivers, and yet true;

9. as unknown, and yet well known; as dying, and behold we live; as chastened, and yet not killed;
10. as sorrowful, yet always rejoicing; as poor, yet making many rich; as having nothing, and yet possessing all things.

INNER COURT RENEWAL

As we allow God to heal us in the Outer Court Process, we can begin our approach to the Inner Court Renewal. In the above scripture, Paul not only gives us the oppositions encountered, but also tells us to commend ourselves with different attributes and characteristics that should encourage and motivate us not to give up in ministry, and to help us keep the faith so that we can be mature, complete and lacking nothing. This truly is a minister who is "Without Blemish".

When we are renewed by the Word of God, we can minister in the Holy Place, and receive illumination from the Lampstand. We can partake of the Bread of His Presence and receive strength and provision to do the things God has called us to do. We can receive the anointing to pray and intercede for others at the Altar of Incense, and we can enjoy 'WORSHIP' and fellowship with the Father in the Holy of Holies. Amen!

CHAPTER 11

Preaching to the Choir
The Talent

I chose this subject last, because in this day and time, talent seems to be most at the forefront. Remember, God is interested in the _heart_ of worship more than the _talent_ of worship. As a praise and worship leader, talent is an important part of worship, however, a talented voice is not necessary to worship God; all is needed is a humble, reverential heart.

There were certain people in the Bible that God specifically appointed as worship leaders and gave them the skill and ability to excel because God commanded it to be so. Chenaniah was one of them. You can say that he held the office of Choir Director, Worship Pastor, or Minister of Music.

I Chronicles 15:22
"Chenaniah, leader of the Levites, was instructor in charge of the music, because he was skillful."

He is again mentioned in verse 27 as the Music Master who led the musicians and singers as the Ark of the Covenant was carried to the City of David.

The Bible says that Chenaniah was skillful. God is a God of excellence. He does not do anything in mediocrity, which means that we as choir members should take our gifting and talents very seriously. There is nothing wrong in taking voice lessons, or music lessons—making sure that we are on top of our game, spiritually and physically; however, God should receive "<u>ALL</u>" the glory through the talents He has given us, whether we are a singer, musician, or dancer.

In keeping this motive, you can *let your light so shine before men, that they may see your good works and glorify your Father in heaven.* **Matthew 5:16**

A PRAYER

Heavenly Father, I come to You in Jesus' Name. I give honor to You, and give thanks for Your Son, Jesus Christ.

I confess my sins to You now. Wash away my sins that I might be whiter than snow; cleanse my heart that I might sing Your praises. Create in me a clean heart, and renew a right spirit within me. I worship You in spirit and truth.

Thank You for choosing me to be used in praise and worship. I give my heart and talents to You to be used through the power of the Holy Spirit. May I bring glory to Your Name to usher Your Presence in the Sanctuary.

In Jesus' Name,

Prepare to Carry His Presence

How shall we bring the Presence of God in?
With steadfast devotion and sanctification.

How shall we carry the Presence which
House the Holy Things of God?

The burden has been placed upon our shoulders.

For we are worshipers with a joyful heart----------
Gladly singing, dancing and praising our God
With musical instruments of Praise!

We shall prepare Him a habitation of worship
For God, in the midst of us, is mighty!

I Chronicles 13:8
And David and all Israel played before God with all their might, and with singing, and with harps, and with psalteries, and with timbrels and with cymbals, and with trumpets.

I Chronicles 15:27-28
And David was clothed with a robe of fine linen, and all the Levites who bore the ark, and the singers, and Chenaniah, the master of the song, with the singers. David also had upon him an ephod of linen.

Thus all Israel brought up the Ark of the Covenant of the Lord with shouting, and with sound of the cornet, and with trumpets, and with cymbals, making a noise with psalteries and harps.

CHAPTER 12

Devotional

<u>The Journal of Selah</u>
(Selah means pause and think of that)

(30 Days of Praise & Worship)

DAY 1

<u>Morning Praise:</u>
Praise the Lord! For it is good to sing praises to our God; for it is pleasant, and praise is beautiful.

Psalm 147:1

Journal of Selah – What is God saying to you?

_____

_____

_____

_____

_____

_____

_____

_____

_____

<u>Evening Worship:</u>
Oh, come, let us worship and bow down; let us kneel before the LORD our maker.

Psalm 95:6

Journal of Selah – What is God saying to you?

_____

_____

_____

_____

_____

_____

_____

_____

DAY 2

<u>Morning Praise</u>:
Sing praises to God, sing praises! Sing praises to our King, sing praises!
For God is the King of all the Earth; sing praises with understanding.
Psalm 47:6-7

Journal of Selah – What is God saying to you?

_____

_____

_____

_____

_____

_____

_____

_____

<u>Evening Worship</u>:
Exalt the LORD our God, And Worship at His footstool—He is holy.
Psalm 99:5

Journal of Selah – What is God saying to you?

_____

_____

_____

_____

_____

_____

_____

_____

203

DAY 3

<u>Morning Praise</u>:
I will praise You, for You have answered me, and have become my salvation.

Psalm 118:21

Journal of Selah – What is God saying to you?

_____

_____

_____

_____

_____

_____

_____

_____

<u>Evening Worship:</u>
I will worship toward Your holy temple, and praise Your Name, for Your lovingkindness and Your truth; for You have magnified Your word above all Your name.

Psalm 138:2

Journal of Selah – What is God Saying to you?

_____

_____

_____

_____

_____

_____

_____

_____

DAY 4

<u>Morning Praise</u>:
All the kings of the earth shall praise You, O LORD, when they hear the words of Your mouth. Yes, they shall sing of the ways of the LORD, for great is the glory of the LORD.

Psalm 138:4-5

Journal of Selah – What is God saying to you?

_____

_____

_____

_____

_____

_____

_____

_____

<u>Evening Worship</u>:
O LORD, You have searched me and known me. You know my sitting down and my rising up. You understand my thought afar off. You comprehend my path and my lying down, and are acquainted with all my ways.

Psalm 139:1-3

Journal of Selah – What is God saying to you?

_____

_____

_____

_____

_____

_____

_____

DAY 5

<u>Morning Praise</u>:
I will praise You, for I am fearfully and wonderfully made; Marvelous are Your works, and that my soul knows very well.

Psalm 138:14

Journal of Selah – What is God saying to you?

_____
_____
_____
_____
_____
_____
_____
_____

<u>Evening Worship</u>:
How precious also are Your thoughts to me, O God! How great is the sum of them! If I should count them, they would be more in number than the sand.

Psalm 139:17-18

Journal of Selah – What is God saying to you?

_____
_____
_____
_____
_____
_____
_____

DAY 6

Morning Praise:
Search me, O God, and know my heart; Try me, and know my anxieties; and see if there is any wicked way in me, and lead me in the way everlasting.

Psalm 139:23-24

Journal of Selah – What is God saying to you?

_____
_____
_____
_____
_____
_____
_____
_____

Evening Worship:
Let my prayer be set before You as incense, the lifting up of my hands as the evening sacrifice.

Psalm 141:2

Journal of Selah – What is God saying to you?

_____
_____
_____
_____
_____
_____
_____
_____

DAY 7

Morning Praise:
Great is the LORD, and greatly to be praised; and His greatness is unsearchable. One generation shall praise Your works to another, and shall declare Your mighty acts.

Psalm 145:3-4

Journal of Selah – What is God saying to you?

_____
_____
_____
_____
_____
_____
_____
_____
_____

Evening Worship:
I will meditate on the glorious splendor of Your majesty, and on Your wondrous works.

Psalm 145:5

Journal of Selah – What is God saying to you?

_____
_____
_____
_____
_____
_____
_____
_____

DAY 8

Morning Praise:

I will extol You, my God, O King, and I will bless Your name forever and ever. Every day I will bless You, and I will praise Your name forever and ever.

Psalm 145:1-2

Journal of Selah – What is God saying to you?

_____

_____

_____

_____

_____

_____

_____

_____

Evening Worship:

"And Moses said to Aaron, This is what the LORD spoke, saying: 'By those who come near Me I must be regarded as holy; and before all the people I must be glorified.' So Aaron held his peace."

Leviticus 10:3

Journal of Selah – What is God saying to you?

_____

_____

_____

_____

_____

_____

_____

_____

DAY 9

Oh, sing to the LORD a new song! For He has done marvelous things; His right hand and His holy arm have gained Him the victory.
Psalm 98:1

Journal of Selah – What is God saying to you?

_____

_____

_____

_____

_____

_____

_____

Evening Worship:
"Oh, worship the LORD in the beauty of holiness! Tremble before Him, all the earth. Say among the nations, 'The LORD reigns; the world also is firmly established, it shall not be moved. He shall judge the peoples righteously.'"
Psalm 96:9-10

Journal of Selah – What is God saying to you?

_____

_____

_____

_____

_____

_____

_____

_____

DAY 10

<u>Morning Praise:</u>
Sing to the LORD with thanksgiving; Sing praises on the harp to our God, Who covers the heavens with clouds, Who prepares rain for the earth, Who makes grass to grow on the mounts.
Psalm 147:7-8

Journal of Selah – What is God saying to you?

_____
_____
_____
_____
_____
_____
_____
_____

<u>Evening Worship:</u>
"When you said, 'Seek My face,' My heart said to You, 'Your face, LORD, I will seek.'"
Psalm 27:8

Journal of Selah – What is God saying to you?

_____
_____
_____
_____
_____
_____
_____
_____

DAY 11

Morning Praise:
The LORD is my strength and my shield; my heart trusted in Him, and I am helped; therefore my heart greatly rejoices, and with my song I will praise Him.

Psalm 28:7

Journal of Selah – What is God saying to you?

_____

_____

_____

_____

_____

_____

_____

Evening Worship:
Blessed are You, LORD God of Israel, our Father, forever and ever. Yours, O LORD, is the greatness, the power and the glory, the victory and the majesty; for all that is in heaven and in earth is Yours; Yours is the kingdom, O LORD, and You are exalted as head over all.

I Chronicles 29:10-11

Journal of Selah – What is God saying to you?

_____

_____

_____

_____

_____

_____

_____

DAY 12

<u>Morning Praise</u>:
Praise the Lord! Praise, O servants of the LORD, Praise the name of the LORD! Blessed be the name of the LORD from this time forth and forevermore! From the rising of the sun to its going down the LORD's name is to be praised.

Psalm 113:1-3

Journal of Selah – What is God saying to you?

_____

_____

_____

_____

_____

_____

_____

_____

<u>Evening Worship</u>:
O LORD, how manifold are Your works! In wisdom You have made them all. The earth is full of Your possessions – This great and wide sea, in which are innumerable teeming things, living things both small and great.

Psalm 104:24-25

Journal of Selah – What is God saying to you?

_____

_____

_____

_____

_____

_____

_____

DAY 13

Morning Praise:

The dead do not praise the LORD, nor any who go down into silence. But we will bless the LORD from this time forth and forevermore. Praise the LORD!

Psalm 115:17-18

Journal of Selah – What is God saying to you?

_____

_____

_____

_____

_____

_____

_____

_____

Evening Worship:

I love the LORD, because He has heard my voice and my supplications. Because He has inclined His ear to me, therefore I will call upon Him as long as I live.

Psalm 116:1

Journal of Selah – What is God saying to you?

_____

_____

_____

_____

_____

_____

_____

_____

DAY 14

Morning Praise:
You are my God, and I will praise You; You are my God, I will exalt You. O give thanks to the LORD, for He is good! For His mercy endures forever.
Psalm 118:28-29

Journal of Selah – What is God saying to you?

_____

_____

_____

_____

_____

_____

_____

_____

Evening Worship:
Teach me, O LORD, the way of Your statues, and I shall keep it to the end. Give me understanding, and I shall keep Your law; Indeed, I shall observe it with my whole heart.
Psalm 119:33-34

Journal of Selah – What is God saying to you?

_____

_____

_____

_____

_____

_____

_____

215

DAY 15

I will lift up my eyes to the hills—from whence comes my help? My help comes from the LORD, who made heaven and earth. He will not allow your foot to be moved; He who keeps you will not slumber. Behold, He who keeps Israel shall neither slumber nor sleep.
Psalm 121:1-5

Journal of Selah – What is God saying to you?

_____
_____
_____
_____
_____
_____
_____

Evening Worship:

Unto You I lift up my eyes, O You who dwell in the heavens. Behold, as the eyes of servants look to the hand of their masters, as the eyes of a maid to the hand of her mistress, so our eyes look to the LORD our God, until He has mercy on us.
Psalm 123:1-2

Journal of Selah – What is God saying to you?

_____
_____
_____
_____
_____
_____
_____

DAY 16

Oh, clap your hands, all you peoples! Shout to God with the voice of triumph! For the LORD Most High is awesome; He is a great King over all the earth.

Psalm 47:1-2

Journal of Selah – What is God saying to you?

_____

_____

_____

_____

_____

_____

_____

_____

Evening Worship:
So the King will greatly desire your beauty; Because He is your Lord, worship Him.

Psalm 45:11

Journal of Selah – What is God saying to you?

_____

_____

_____

_____

_____

_____

_____

_____

DAY 17

Morning Praise:
My mouth shall speak the praise of the LORD, and all flesh shall bless His holy name forever, and ever.

Psalm 145:21

Journal of Selah – What is God saying to you?

_____

_____

_____

_____

_____

_____

_____

_____

Evening Worship:
The Twenty-four elders fall down before Him who sit on the throne and worship Him who live forever and ever, and cast their crowns before the throne, saying: You are worthy, O Lord, to receive glory and honor and power; For you created all things, and by Your will they exist and were created.

Revelation 4:10-11

Journal of Selah – What is God saying to you?

_____

_____

_____

_____

_____

_____

_____

_____

DAY 18

Morning Praise:
Bless the LORD, O my soul! O LORD my God, You are very great; You are clothed with honor and majesty, Who cover Yourself with light as with a garment, Who stretch out the heavens like a curtain.
Psalm 104:1-2

Journal of Selah – What is God saying to you?

_____

_____

_____

_____

_____

_____

_____

Evening Worship:
The Lord is merciful and gracious; slow to anger, and abounding in mercy. He will not always strive with us, nor will He keep His anger forever. He has not dealt with us according to our sins, nor punished us according to our iniquities.
Psalm 103:8-10

Journal of Selah – What is God saying to you?

_____

_____

_____

_____

_____

_____

_____

DAY 19

Morning Praise:

Oh, give thanks to the LORD! Call upon His name; Make known His deeds among the peoples! Sing to Him, sing psalms to Him; talk of all His wondrous works! Glory in His holy name; let the hearts of those rejoice who seek the Lord!

Psalm 105:1-3

Journal of Selah – What is God saying to you?

_____

_____

_____

_____

_____

_____

_____

Evening Worship:

All the angles stood around the throne and the elders and the four living creatures, and fell on their faces before the throne and worshiped God, saying: Amen! Blessing and glory and wisdom, thanksgiving and honor and power and might, be to our God forever and ever. Amen.

Revelation 7:11-12

Journal of Selah – What is God saying to you?

_____

_____

_____

_____

_____

_____

DAY 20

<u>Morning Praise</u>:
Behold; bless the LORD, all you servants of the LORD, who by night stand in the house of the LORD! Lift up your hands in the sanctuary, and bless the LORD. The LORD who made heaven and earth bless you from Zion!

Psalm 134:1-3

Journal of Selah – What is God saying to you?

_____
_____
_____
_____
_____
_____
_____
_____

<u>Evening Worship</u>:
For I know that the LORD is great and our Lord is above all gods. Whatever the LORD pleases He does, in heaven and in earth.

Psalm 135:5-6

Journal of Selah – What is God saying to you?

_____
_____
_____
_____
_____
_____
_____
_____

DAY 21

<u>Morning Praise</u>:
I will praise the Lord according to his righteousness and will sing praise to the Name of the Lord Most High.
Psalm 7:17

Journal of Selah – What is God saying to you?

_____

_____

_____

_____

_____

_____

_____

_____

<u>Evening Worship:</u>
Bless the LORD, O my soul; and all that is within me, bless His holy Name! Bless the LORD, O my soul, and forget not all His benefits; Who forgives all your iniquities, Who heals all your diseases, Who redeems your life from destruction, Who crowns you with lovingkindness and tender mercies.
Psalm 103:1-3

Journal of Selah – What is God saying to you?

_____

_____

_____

_____

_____

_____

DAY 22

Morning Praise:

PRAISE the LORD! Sing to the LORD a new song, and His praise in the assembly of saints. Let Israel rejoice in their Maker; Let the children of Zion be joyful in their King.

Psalm 149:1-2

Journal of Selah – What is God saying to you?

_____

_____

_____

_____

_____

_____

_____

_____

Evening Worship:

And the twenty-four elders who sat before God on their thrones fell on their faces and worshiped God, saying: We give You thanks, O Lord God Almighty, The One who is and who was and who is to come, because You have taken Your great power and reigned.

Revelation 11:16-17

Journal of Selah – What is God saying to you?

_____

_____

_____

_____

_____

_____

_____

_____

DAY 23

Morning Praise:

Morning Praise:
Let them praise His name with the dance; let them sing praises to Him with the timbrel and harp. For the LORD takes pleasure in His people; He will beautify the humble with salvation.
                    Psalm 149:3-4

Journal of Selah – What is God saying to you?

_____

_____

_____

_____

_____

_____

_____

_____

Evening Worship:
Who shall not fear You, O Lord, and glorify Your name? For You alone are holy. For all nations shall come and worship before You, for Your judgments have been manifested.
                    Revelation 15:4

Journal of Selah – What is God saying to you?

_____

_____

_____

_____

_____

_____

_____

_____

DAY 24

Morning Praise:
Let the saints be joyful in glory; Let them sing aloud on their beds. Let the high praises of God be in their mouth, and a two-edged sword in their hand.

Psalm 149:5-6

Journal of Selah – What is God saying to you?

_____

_____

_____

_____

_____

_____

_____

_____

_____

Evening Worship:
"After these things I heard a loud voice of a great multitude in heaven, saying 'Alleluia! Salvation and glory and honor and power belong to the Lord our God'!"

Revelation 19:1

Journal of Selah – What is God saying to you?

_____

_____

_____

_____

_____

_____

_____

DAY 25

"The voice came from the throne, saying, 'Praise our God, all you His servants and those who fear Him, both small and great'!"
Revelation 19:5

Journal of Selah – What is God saying to you?

_____
_____
_____
_____
_____
_____
_____
_____
_____

Evening Worship:
"Saying with a loud voice, 'Fear God and give glory to Him, for the hour of His judgment has come; and worship Him who made heaven and earth, the sea and springs of water.'"
Revelation 14:7

Journal of Selah – What is God saying to you?

_____
_____
_____
_____
_____
_____
_____
_____

DAY 26

<u>Morning Praise</u>:
I thank You and praise You, O God of my fathers; You have given me wisdom and might, and have now made known to me what we asked of You.

Daniel 2:23

Journal of Selah – What is God saying to you?

_____

_____

_____

_____

_____

_____

_____

_____

<u>Evening Worship</u>:
Teach me to do Your will, for You are my God; Your Spirit is good. Lead me in the land of uprightness.

Psalm 143:10

Journal of Selah – What is God saying to you?

_____

_____

_____

_____

_____

_____

_____

_____

DAY 27

<u>Morning Praise</u>:
PRAISE the LORD! Praise God in His sanctuary; Praise Him in His mighty firmament! Praise Him for His mighty acts; Praise Him according to His excellent greatness!
Psalm 150:1-2

Journal of Selah – What is God saying to you?

_____

_____

_____

_____

_____

_____

_____

_____

<u>Evening Worship</u>:
Give to the LORD the glory due His name; bring an offering, and come before Him. Oh, worship the LORD in the beauty of holiness!
1 Chronicles 16:29

Journal of Selah – What is God saying to you?

_____

_____

_____

_____

_____

_____

_____

_____

DAY 28

Praise Him with the sound of the trumpet; Praise Him with the lute and harp!

Psalm 150:3

Journal of Selah – What is God saying to you?

_____

_____

_____

_____

_____

_____

_____

_____

Evening Worship:
"Tremble before Him, all the earth. The world also is firmly estab-lished, it shall not be moved. Let the heavens rejoice, and let the earth be glad; and let them say among the nations, 'The LORD reigns!'"

I Chronicles 16:30-31

Journal of Selah – What is God saying to you?

_____

_____

_____

_____

_____

_____

_____

_____

DAY 29

Praise Him with the timbrel and dance; Praise Him with stringed instruments and flutes! Praise Him with loud cymbals; praise Him with clashing cymbals! Let everything that has breath praise the LORD. Praise the LORD!

Psalm 150:4-6

Journal of Selah – What is God saying to you?

_____

_____

_____

_____

_____

_____

_____

_____

Evening Worship:

"'And now, behold, I have brought the firstfruits of the land which you, O LORD, have given me.' Then you shall set it before the LORD your God, and worship before the LORD your God."

Deuteronomy 26:10

Journal of Selah – What is God saying to you?

_____

_____

_____

_____

_____

_____

_____

DAY 30

<u>Morning Praise</u>:
Sing to the LORD, all the earth; proclaim the good news of His salvation from day to day. Declare His glory among the nations, His wonders among all peoples. For the LORD is great and greatly to be praised; He is also to be feared above all gods.
I Chronicles 16:23-25

Journal of Selah – What is God saying to you?

_____
_____
_____
_____
_____
_____
_____
_____
_____

<u>Evening Worship:</u>
Now we know that God does not hear sinners; but if anyone is a worshiper of God and does His will, He hears him.
John 9:31

Journal of Selah – What is God saying to you?

_____
_____
_____
_____
_____
_____
_____

CPSIA information can be obtained
at www.ICGtesting.com
Printed in the USA
BVOW08s1605271017
498816BV00001B/74/P